The Saint

Brown University Press Providence

The Saint

By Conrad Ferdinand Meyer

A Fictional Biography
of Thomas Becket
Translated from the German
by W. F. Twaddell

Brown University Press

Providence, Rhode Island 02912

English translation © 1977 by Brown University

All rights reserved

Set in VIP Trump by G&S Typesetters, Inc.

Printed in the United States of America

By Halliday Lithograph Corporation

On Warren's Olde Style

Bound by Halliday Lithograph Corporation

Designed by Richard Hendel

Library of Congress Cataloging in Publication Data:

Meyer, Conrad Ferdinand, 1825–1898.
  The saint.

  Translation of Der Heilige.
    1. Thomas à Becket, Saint, Abp. of Canterbury,
1118?–1170—Fiction.   I. Title.
PZ3.M574Sai9 [PT2432] 833'.7   77–7038
ISBN 0–87057–149–4

Foreword

CONRAD FERDINAND MEYER was born into a patrician
family in Zürich, 11 October 1825. His youth was clouded
by the death of an adored father in 1840. Meyer's mother,
who had a hereditary tendency to self-distrust and melancholy (she committed suicide in 1856), was a most unfortunate influence during his adolescence and early adult
life. Although the devotion of his younger sister Betsy
was a constant support, he suffered from serious depres-
sions. He spent several weeks in 1852 under medical care;
intelligent and affectionate treatment soon brought about
a balance. From this time, his literary production, which
had been tentative and essentially private, shows increasing confidence. Even so, it was only in his forties that
mastery of lyric and dramatic poetry was confirmed by his
own critical judgment and the beginnings of public recognition. Soon he started to publish prose narratives. During
his later forties, through his fifties, and into his sixties, a
succession of novels and *Novellen* appeared. Meyer died
28 November 1898, after several years of failing mental
powers.

Meyer ranks among the half-dozen major German poets
and prose writers of the nineteenth century. His work is
characterized by refinement of style and meticulous construction, whether of plot or of lyric design. He is a master
of the salient detail. His prose narratives are without exception set in the past; in them, the records of historical
events and personages are given body and motivation
through vivid portrayal and psychological insights. The

v

narratives explore problems of identity, of impulse and constraint, of individual will and the limitations imposed by the community or by accident, of *malum prohibitum* and *malum in se*.

Der Heilige (The Saint) was published in 1880. It is a work of assured maturity and seriousness. An underlying irony is muted but present throughout. The story of two characters, potentially complementary and deeply incompatible, is narrated against a background of superficial decorum and ruthless realities. Meyer controls the impact of events through the device of the frame-narrative. The scene of the telling is the suite of a canon of the Zürich Grossmünster; the narrator is a simple-seeming observer-participant who combines Upper Rhine Valley and Muslim insights; the hearer is a sophisticated-seeming cleric. The narrator knows guilt and folly—his own and others'—and has been strong enough to survive. The hearer has observed human life, shrewdly but from a shelter. Meyer's reader is shown something of the mystery of personality and chance, presented with understanding pity but without sentimentality.

In Meyer's narratives a set of historical human beings, their deeds and their fates are the starting point from which he develops a meaningful work of fiction. Meyer does not write or rewrite history, but historical novels; the product of his pen is literature, not research scholarship. Of the attested facts he uses what he needs for a coherent work of art and does not hesitate to omit, alter, or add, either in detail or in fairly basic components of the story he has to tell. In this novella dealing with Thomas Becket he manipulates chronology, incorporates a late thirteenth-century legend which represents the mother of Thomas as a Saracen emir's daughter and then expands this motif by creating a decisively important Muslim background for Becket's youth, treats the characters of King Henry and Queen Eleanor so that they fit into his requirements for the story, invents a daughter who has a passive but crucial role, and sets the entire narrative about Thomas within a fictional framework.

Readers who are interested in Meyer's freedom in using historical records may compare *The Saint* with the book that was his immediate stimulus: *Histoire de la conquête de l'Angleterre par les Normands*, by Augustin Thierry

(1795–1856). Those interested in the historical Thomas Becket can refer to brief articles in the *Columbia Encyclopedia* and in the *Encyclopaedia Britannica*. A fuller account, by Kate Norgate, is provided in the *Dictionary of National Biography*. There is a readable popular biography, *Thomas Becket of Canterbury*, by Alfred Duggan (1952). Nesta Pain's *The King and Becket* (1964) narrates the development of the controversies between the monarch and the archbishop, focusing upon the strengths and weaknesses of Thomas's defense of ecclesiastical privileges, and his strategies and tactics as he fought for them.

During the past century two major works of English literature have treated aspects of the Thomas Becket theme. Tennyson's *Becket* (1884) was staged with considerable success (first performance 6 February 1893) with Henry Irving and Ellen Terry in lead roles. T. S. Eliot's *Murder in the Cathedral* (1935) focuses on the inner drama of the martyrdom. Neither Tennyson nor Eliot appears to have made use of Meyer's work, or indeed to have been aware of it.

THROUGHOUT THE drafting of this translation, Dr. Antonia Degen Warren has given invaluable help. In addition to being a native speaker of the language of the novel, with almost a native speaker's mastery of English, Mrs. Warren is thoroughly familiar with Meyer's native city and its culture, since her childhood and her younger years were spent in Zürich, the scene of her education up through the medical doctorate. During all stages of the work, she contributed linguistic, geographical, and historical insights. The completed translation is very much the better for this help, which is acknowledged with warm thanks.

The publication of this translation has been aided by the award of a generous grant by the Pro Helvetia foundation of Zürich.

W.F.T.

The Saint

Chapter One

THE SLOWLY falling snow was covering the open countryside and the roofs of isolated farmhouses on both sides
of the military highway which leads from the warm spas
on the Limmat to Zürich, a free city, sovereign within the
Holy Roman Empire. The flakes were floating down more
and more densely, as if to obliterate the pallid morning
light and bring the world to a halt, overspreading highway
and byway and whatever was moving on them.

Now muffled hoofbeats pounded hollowly on the
planking of the covered bridge across the Sihl not far from
the city, and a single rider came into view under the raf-
ters of the gloomy opening toward the city walls. His
sturdy form was warmly wrapped in a rough woolen
cloak, and he had pulled the hood up over his head, so that
scarcely more of him than a broad gray beard was visible.
Close behind the horse, which was of a local breed, a big
poodle trotted along, its back covered with snow and its
tail drooping in melancholy. The reverberation of the
hoofbeats in the wooden passageway roused the three
travelers from the half-sleep into which cold and snow
had lulled them, and held out the expectation of the city
gate and shelter nearby. The gate was reached in a quick
trot. As they passed under the low arch the rider pushed
back his riding hood, shook some snowflakes from his
cloak, and rode in good posture, military despite the burden of his years, through the Rennweg, the first street
along the foot of the imperial residence.

It was the twenty-ninth of December in the year of

grace 1191. It was the traveler's custom to pay a visit to Zürich between Christmas and the year's end.

On the right the baker had his fresh loaves ready; on the left, under the sooty overhanging roof of the smithy, the anvil was resounding and sparks were spraying. From right and left the rider was welcomed today, as he always was when he came to Zürich, and noisily greeted as "Hans the Armorer" or "Hans the Englishman." But the broad Alemannic sounds with which he returned the greetings came so naturally from his mouth that the second name could scarcely refer to a faraway homeland but rather to a fondness for travel and venturesome journeyings that had been satisfied. Curious about the hoofbeats, the innkeeper at the sign of the Lion came to his doorway; he recognized the passing rider, raised his cap, and asked how this year's Schaffhauser wine was behaving in the storage cellars. The rider's answer was so well informed and revealed such concern with the question that it was not hard to infer where the crops of the "Englishman" grew and where his wine was maturing.

Up to this point, Hans the Armorer found everything happening the way he had known it for decades in the city of the princess-abbess. But there was one thing that made an impression of strangeness and that he gradually began to turn over in his mind: This was not a holiday, and in this severe time of year and at this early hour only a few women would normally be moving about out of doors. But today they were crossing thresholds with quick steps and in full finery. As Master Hans rode on through steeply sloping narrow streets toward the center of the city and rode across the bridge over the swift current of the Limmat and past the town hall, it seemed to him that there were parades of ants running upstream along both banks. One group followed another. Women of all ranks— haughty noble ladies with costly missals in their hands, worthy daughters of artisans, modest nuns, pretty girls of a free-and-easy way of life—hurried on alongside wrinkled coughing grandmothers who had pulled their cloaks up over their poor gray heads against the snow flurries. They were all streaming toward the lake, where the minsters stood, like the helmets of two knights, at the outlet into the Limmat.

But, what did that mean? From only one of them, the

Minster of Our Lady, bells were sending out the church's urgent invitation; the Great Minster across from it persisted in disapproving silence.

The armorer rode on thoughtfully, following the procession. He rode under the arches, up along the Limmat toward the famed inn at the sign of Saint Meinrad's Ravens, where he was accustomed to stay every year. But now, at the foot of the hill where once the blood of Saint Felix and Saint Regula had been shed, he stopped his bay. He had glanced up into the steep Church Street that ends here, leading down from the Great Minster. There he caught sight of an elegant, venerable, marten-clad canon walking toward him, carefully choosing the best places in the melting snow. His face seemed pale under the black biretta. He was looking at his soaked shoes with a pained expression; for that reason he was not immediately aware of the armorer, who had vigorously swung out of the saddle and was waiting for the old gentleman in a respectful posture, head bared despite the continuing snow shower.

"The grace of God and His mother upon you, reverend sire," was the greeting of Hans the Englishman when the old gentleman came alongside him. In some surprise the canon fixed a shrewd eye on the greeter, and a sudden sign of recognition flitted across his pale features—apparently a pleasant but craftily restrained recognition.

So it was the armorer who started the conversation: "Permit me to ask if I will find your worthy brother, the noble Sir Kuno, in the collegiate church. He owes me a small sum for some crossbows I made, and also the cost of an item built in the English style that was ordered and delivered three years ago. I would like to collect it all before the new year, according to my practice. During the Christmas season last year and the year before that I encountered the noble gentleman with his resources exhausted, since he had had to contend with persistent misfortune at dice. How may things be standing with him this year?"

"That you must ask him yourself, after we have shared a meal," was the reply. "He will be back at the church this evening. All of the brethren have gone hunting, prior and the whole chapter, with the exception of an old man like me. I had in mind devoting some of my time outside the monastery to the new saint whose martyrdom and

5

miracles are being expounded to the faithful believers over there (he gestured toward the soaring choir of Our Lady's minster) by a clever preacher from Lucerne—and whose halo has banished from the city for today those brothers of mine who are unreasonably sensitive about it. But since it was curiosity more than piety that guided my steps and since heaven's snow is hindering them, I may turn back with no harm to my soul.

"Let them take your horse to the inn at the sign of the Ravens. The stable boy of Saint Meinrad's is standing there by the river as if he had taken root and is staring across at Our Lady's minster. Your Tapp can warm himself at my kitchen fire instead of sitting here dismally in the snow. As for me, by the bleeding head of Saint Felix, I can't stand here in this dripping wet any longer! The insidious witch with the tongs sits here in these icy puddles. I mean that miserable gout that has been giving me twinges this winter and has only recently let up on me. Follow me, Englishman!"

After these eloquent words Sir Burkhard wrapped himself with a shiver in his fur and began the ascent of the wet street, just as circumspectly as he had come.

Hans summoned the lounging hostler and turned over to him the reins along with all kinds of orders, and gave him instructions for the innkeeper to pass on to the regular customers at the Ravens. For the nobility patronized it, and among the noblemen the armorer had a number of clients and debtors.

Then he unbuckled his knapsack from the animal's back and took the baggage under his arm. He strode up the street leading to the chapter church with Tapp, who was inseparable from his master's property.

Hans welcomed the canon's invitation. Hans the Armorer was a frugal man.

Chapter Two

THE WINTRY DAY continued so dark that the hospitable canon's narrow room was lighted more by the flickering gold of flames in the hearth than by the one little window up near the ceiling.

While the armorer was finishing his meal, Sir Burkhard, who was physically fastidious and moderate in his way of life, had already been sitting back in his fleece-covered armchair, his feet wrapped in a fur blanket and stretched toward the fire. The table was cleared by an equally aged steward, who put a jug of strong local wine and two silver goblets on the stone mantel of the fireplace.

The canon was obviously in a cheerful mood. It gratified him that on this gloomy wintry day he had lured into his quarters a quick-witted, widely traveled man who knew the world and human nature and was especially qualified to throw light on some matters that the canon had long been curious about. The finely shaped head with its few snow-white strands lay on the red cushion of the chairback; his eyes were closed, but there was an alert expression of triumph for his successful ruse.

Now he suddenly opened his eyes and beamed at the armorer: "Blessings on the meal, Hans! Turn your chair and move over here to me. You asked me who that new saint is who is exalted by the ladies at the minster but belittled by us canons. I don't think it is wholesome to discuss ecclesiastical or theological matters at mealtime. But now I am ready to give information.

"The new mediator in heaven whom the Holy Father of

Christendom has bestowed on us saw the light of day the same year as I did. That fact alone speaks against him. The same rule holds good for saints and for wine: the older the better and the more efficacious. Just as this (he took a sip from his goblet) is the blood of our soil, akin to our blood to which it has given zest and strength from time immemorial, so likewise our Saint Felix and Saint Regula, above whose bodies this monastery and this city are built, continue to exercise their power. As mighty helpers in time of need they have watched over generation after generation. We are familiar with them, beholden to them; and they are familiar with us and beholden to us. We validate our acts with the seal of Zürich which bears their picture, as our forefathers have done. I don't want to boast about the documented fact that after their bloody martyrdom by decapitation at the bank of the Limmat they carried their severed heads in their own hands forty steps uphill to this spot—although certainly none of these puny recent saints could equal that miracle. For me it is worth recalling that the blood of Saint Felix and Saint Regula bore witness to their faith against a pagan emperor, that they did not presumptuously rebel against a Christian king and liege lord, as this new saint, my contemporary, did.

"But the heads of the ladies of the princely convent are incapable of such ponderings. Fate had it that among other costly manuscripts a parchment describing and glorifying the life and martyrdom of my contemporary fell into their hands. The sacred documents were read aloud for edification during meals, and from then on the thoughts of the noble women found no rest. They urged openly and brought secret pressures to bear to have the day of the martyr celebrated here.

"Whatever is novel and exotic appeals to women. Our town council was averse to the proposal for the reasons I mentioned and would have put a stop to the whole thing except for the fact that a favorable act of Heaven came to the ladies' aid.

"Last September during a long dry spell one of the abbey's barns at their large farmhouse in Wiedikon, stored full of hay, caught fire. The hot breezes of the foehn were driving the flames directly toward the farm manager's house, which was beginning to smoke and seemed lost.

Then Lady Berta, the formidably pious administrator of the estate, had the farmer and his sons drag a heavy slate board in front of the house. She took a piece of chalk and wrote on the slab in letters as long as your arm: 'Saint Thomas, help us!'

"What happened? Did the saint look down from heaven and read the plea? Be that as it may, instantly the wind shifted, the barn collapsed in a pile of dying embers, the farmhouse was saved. At this moment help arrived from the city. Here was the blackboard, yonder the heap of charred debris; there was no arguing against the miracle and the saint.

"Thus it has come about that today we celebrate the feast day—the day, I must not forget to mention, of Saint Thomas of Canterbury."

After this detailed account the canon grasped his tankard and took several sips. He picked up the jug and glanced toward the listener, to fill his goblet. Hans, sitting on a wooden footstool by the fire, made no sound. Something strange had been happening to him. At first he had attentively followed the canon's narration, his elbows braced on his knees and with lowered head. Sir Burkhard had purposely not given the saint's name until the very end, but the armorer had probably guessed it before that. Now he remained motionless as if inwardly crushed, and it seemed as though he shivered and shook all over. The canon poured him a full goblet and studied him, looking at him sympathetically, with just a gleam of mischievous malice showing through.

"At last I have caught you, you sly fellow! By the bloody braids of Saint Regula, Armorer, today you won't step back over my threshold without having told me what you know about Saint Thomas of Canterbury, and quite different things from what the Lucerne parson is imposing on the credulity of the ladies over at the convent or what is written in the parchment which the noble prioress has lent me for the healing of my soul. You met the saint during the days of his earthly life, you won't deny that! I heard how you declared—it is probably just about a year ago now—to my brother canons over there in our commons room, loudly and with expansive gestures —for they had plied you vigorously with the cup—that you lived as close to King Henry as the button of his

9

jacket, indeed as the skin to his body. You were worked up to a fiery passion, for my brethren had expressed their doubts that King Henry had shed tears of joy on the occasion of that ill-fated coronation of his oldest son. You shouted: 'I saw them flow!' and swore it by the salvation of your soul. I was just about to enter to drink a social cup (for I was then that much younger), and I heard you affirm your story with an oath, and I believed you, because you are not a braggart. But if you were constantly in the presence of King Henry, if you handed him garment and goblet, if you knew his laughing and his weeping, as you asserted, then you must also have known the man who destroyed him body and soul—either while serving him as chancellor, or later as a holy bishop, his enemy and his victim, driving him to despair and destruction. Perhaps, unfortunate man, you were among those who assisted the saint to his martyrdom. But no! It is recorded in the abbess's parchment that the killers of the saint lost their claim to being human to such an extent that their dogs refused food from their hands. And Tapp"—he pointed to the poodle head which was pressed forward attentively between the armorer's knees—"Tapp, as I have seen, accepts everything that you offer him."

"God's grace preserved me from that," Hans murmured. "But the saint, yes, I knew him as well as I know you, Sir Burkhard. And, if you must know it, I was there when William Tracy split his skull in front of the high altar. And I still see his smile—God forgive me for saying it—the holy, mocking smile with which he perished, as if the headsman were doing him a service of love. O sir, those are heavy, inscrutable events."

"Tell the story, Hans," said the canon in a voice tremulous with expectation. He straightened up, bracing his old hands on the arms of his chair.

The armorer stirred the fire and silently pulled his thoughts together. His firm, angular features had grown somber, and his sparkling eyes were thoughtful. He obviously found it reasonable that he should grant his host's request, but he did so reluctantly. For those events, which were just as amazing and incomprehensible for the participants as for outsiders, were the most significant part of the story of his own life. It was not easy for the reserved man to talk about those events; it reached down into the depths of his being where his feelings were ambiguous and his thoughts halted at the brink of a precipice.

He spoke warily: "It may well be, Sir Burkhard, that you are better informed about the royal transactions and deeds of my lord the king in the affairs of the world. But as for his way of life and his nature—and as for the human countenance of Thomas Becket—" he added softly and timidly, "truly I was no braggart on that drunken night a year ago when I boasted that I knew them well, although it would have been better for me to have kept silent. Even today, sir, I need only shut my eyes to see both king and priest before me, clear as life. The sight is not as pretty as the vision of those long serene faces which your city's patron saints are carrying here in their hands!" And he pointed toward the central panel of the colored tapestry that covered the wall. "For years, after I had come home from England, those two unhappy men forced themselves into my thoughts by day and my dreams by night. During the day I constantly had to recall the gentle subtle discourse of the one and the frivolous jokes, rough threats, despairing rages of the other; and I was forced to ponder how inevitably disaster for both was growing out of those words. At night I saw them moving headlong against each other amid smoke and flames, as the Apostle John writes in his Revelation. And each of my wives—I have married and buried several—had to share my alarm and horror as she shook me awake. Sir, when kings and saints collide, it is something quite different from what happens when there is yelling and stabbing in our Swabian taverns. But so be it: I will speak to you about those histories. It is a sad thing and hard to master, but I must fulfill the wish of my host," the armorer concluded with a stern smile.

"Then do as you promise," said the canon, settling back in his chair with an expression of lively anticipation.

Chapter Three

HANS THE ENGLISHMAN began his story: "I take no
pleasure in speaking about my youth and avoid thinking
about it, except when I must recall it before the high
festivals to humble myself before God and His Blessed
Mother, or when in my old age some envious foe maliciously flings it into my teeth. But I must burden you and
myself with the account of it, for my poor little career
cannot be separated from that of the saint and of the
king—at least not in my old brain. I must tell you that I
come of a noble family. If you were to say 'Hohenklingen'
or 'Hohenkrähen' you would not name my ancestral
home, which now lies in ruins; but its name would not be
too different, and like those strongholds it was located not
far from Lake Constance and the Rhine.

My father was deeply in debt and—God only knows
why—shunned and disdained by his kindred. To escape
his creditors and save his soul he took the cross and was
off to the Holy Land; he never returned. From my birth
onward my poor mother dragged a sickly body around,
and she wept her heart out when my older brother was
killed, not on the field of chivalric honor but in a sordid
brawl over money. For we made our way as best we could,
lying in wait along highways for whatever came our way.
I made no effort to get advice or help from kinsmen; there
would have been none. My only friends were my crossbow and my dogs, with whom I wandered through the
forest.

I myself was pursued like a hunted animal by an evil

enemy, whom I hated as the very devil. That was Manasse, the Jewish moneylender in Schaffhausen. My father had put up his stable and his few fields as security for a loan. Now it happened that my mother sent me to the Jew to ask for an extension, but there was no mercy in the usurer. Suddenly I was seized by grief and pity for my sick mother, and also for the bloody sufferings of our Savior, whom the Jews had tortured cruelly, and I beat Manasse to death with my fists. May God not hold that killing against me! When I committed that murder, even though I had a man's growth and strength, I was still a child, and I had an impressionable and impetuous disposition.

Manasse had many friends in the city and among the neighboring noblemen, and I would have been lost except for the open door of All Saints' monastery. And since I had every reason to be glad when the door was firmly closed behind me, I unexpectedly became clerical and, after a year's interval, a monk. In that whole matter I acted honorably and without guile; but I was ill fitted to be a monk, and I had not foreseen the way my nature was to grow and the soil in which it would thrive. Do not misunderstand me! I am thinking not only of the sinful blood of our first parents but more of that kindling spark which leapt from the hand of God the Father Creator into the clay of which I am formed: strength, understanding, enterprise, creativity, wanderlust. At All Saints' there was nothing to be learned about human art and science except the poet Vergil, whose work I still know in large measure by heart even today.

The prior extolled this poet as having been a godly heathen and inspired by God with prophetic power as a reward of his virtue, so that in his verses the blessed Mother and Child were reflected and could be clearly recognized.

Thus the scroll from which I studied was full of stiletto holes. On Saint John's Eve, Midsummer Night of the year I left All Saints' and before I went over the wall, I made three augury-seeking stabs after fervent invocation of the three names of the Trinity, and I hit the words *sagittas, calamo, arcui*. And Vergil had spoken truth: arrows and bows have played important parts in my life.

So again I made use of my swift feet and moved rapidly through the hilly forested region toward Alsace, cutting off the great bend of the Rhine in a straight line. Toward noon I came to a meadow in front of a fortress. An archery contest was being held, by all sorts of people. On the way I had already felt a kind of intoxication from the smell of the earth and the joy of using my limbs. So it isn't to be wondered at that in the carnival amid the turmoil of the archers I let the unruly fellows, who were having their fun with the runaway monk, put a bow in my hands. Taking the posture with foot advanced, I put shot after shot into the target. My eyesight, I must tell you, is sharp and clear; it has never failed me since childhood.

I think they got me drunk—I was disused to the goblet —so that in a glow I rolled up my sleeves and hitched the robe up to my thighs. I have an unclear and offensive picture of being carried around with naked arms and legs amid laughter and ridicule in a fool's triumph.

The next morning I hiked on, in a servant's costume that some good fellow gave me. I thought over my condition, with shame. Behind me on the right lay a smirched scutcheon, and a torn monk's robe on the left. There was nothing left for me but manual work, and I cast about for a trade that would not entirely isolate me from knightly people and activities and would furnish a living in war and peace. The Vergilian augury became clear; I resolved to become a bowman and maker of crossbows.

Making a beginning is hard, dear sir, and beside the idle habits of the highwayman and the monk I had many follies of an unformed disposition to overcome. I needed to discover a stable way of life. Although I had already killed a Jew and broken monastic vows, even so my devout sentiments almost plunged me into yet a third misdeed. I will tell you about this, too; for the rest I will be brief.

As I was traveling on foot toward Strassburg, I fell in with a band of wandering scholars. We were carousing in a tavern across from the walls and spires of the famed city. Then I remembered how my mother used to talk a great deal about a pious aunt who led a holy life in a Strassburg cloister. When the waters of misery were rising to her mouth to engulf her, she used to invoke the aunt's intercession in heaven, and with benefit. I thought of doing the same thing, for guidance on my wanderings. Accordingly I addressed myself to one of the travelers, who had a frank and candid face and who said he knew the city well from of old, and asked him as a friend if he couldn't point out to me the cloister where my aunt Willibirg had died in the odor of sanctity.

'My dear fellow,' he answered, 'do you see there the octagonal tower with the colored roof? And beside it the long building next to the city wall? That is where your aunt held sway.'

Then I fell to my knees. Looking across the river at the house, I fervently besought the holy woman to aid me in all good and salutary works. What do I hear behind me? Suppressed giggles, an outburst of raucous laughing. Quickly looking around, I see that the wandering scholar had pulled the corners of his coat into two long ears which he was waving and wagging alongside mine. The others continued their unrestrained laughing, 'The jackass is praying to the fancy ladies' house!' The scoundrel was already under my knees; while heavy tears dropped from my eyes at the unkindness and badness of the world, I was choking him and his life's breath would soon have stopped if the others had not pulled him away from me.

IN STRASSBURG I began my apprenticeship with a bowmaker, who treated me fairly and taught me honestly all the skills of the trade as far as he knew them. But he was a man of custom and habit; he shook his head stubbornly at the improvements and refinements of which the structure and the shape of the crossbow are capable, which at that time were spreading into the Holy Roman Empire from England and Flanders and especially from heathen Granada. But I had the spirit of youth and curiosity, and after a few starts that were quickly surpassed I had no peace. For, dear sir, in even the meanest art lies a hidden goal of perfection which beckons to us and attracts us onward to pursue it ardently day and night.

At that time I often dreamed that I had built a crossbow and shaped a bolt that carried farther than the Saracen weapon. But then in the morning twilight my little discoveries paled like a will-o'-the-wisp. For they were crude fumblings or capricious ideas, since I knew a few artifices but not the fundamentals and laws of my craft.

So I resolved to travel and learn from the masters of the art. I made my way through France and Aquitania and over the Pyrenees. Every evening in the red clouds of sunset I saw the magic city, Granada, toward which my whole being was drawing me, until at last it was truly and actually there before me on the western horizon. And it was granted me to see the world-famed splendor that had been built up there, the arabesque stone screenwork ornamentation of its palaces, the palms and cypresses of its miraculous gardens, the ascending jets of its rustling and murmuring fountains."

"My poor Hans," Sir Burkhard interrupted, "and did you return uncircumcised in body and unshaken in faith?"

"Have no doubt of it—and with a much shrewder head on my shoulders than I had taken there. So far as my Christian faith is concerned, sir canon, I maintained it against a great philosopher, whom I helped perfect the tubes through which he observed the courses of the stars. Night after night he showed me the slowly traveling armies of the sky and expounded to me how from all eternity the destinies of mankind had been bound to those radiant signs and forms, those animal shapes, and balances, so that no human or divine hand could reach into the turning spokes of the fiery wheel; therefore there was no scope for human choice or for God's wrath or favor. But I did not believe him, and I had as my evidence the flood of remorse when I sinned.

In general I discovered and learned in Granada what I had come there to find. It is the simple truth, sir: the heathen bowmakers are unsurpassed. After all, long long ago they derived from the shape of the bow the compact and handy crossbow, as legend has it and as I can readily believe. For God has bestowed on the heathens art and science, mathematics, mechanics, skill in construction —the learnings involved in counting and weighing—in order, as I believe, to grant them a brief hour of pride before their eternal death."

The canon nodded his agreement with these sage words, and the bowman continued: "I spent three years in the heathens' city. The days flew by as my work raced onward; and in the evenings I found pleasure, free from wine and quarreling, in the airy open halls where they used to tell stories. For I was gradually becoming fluent in Arabic. There was one brown lad with fiery eyes whom they loved to listen to, because he knew how to mimic .

the demeanor of both sexes and all ages and classes with a lively play of expression and gesture. From his mouth I once heard a tale that was no better and no worse than the rest. You will think it is beside the point, but I will not omit it, because it is a part of what we are talking about.

It is the story of Prince Moonlight. It tells of a young stranger who came to Cordova from an island in the north and won the favor of the caliph through the magic of his appearance and speech and his masterful skill at chess. Beside that, they say, despite his charming youthfulness he possessed such acuteness of understanding and political wisdom that through his advice the caliph before long had become the mightiest of Moorish kings, without war or bloodshed and solely through diplomacy. Hence he became infatuated with Prince Moonlight—that is what the Cordovans called the foreigner because of his gentleness and the pallor of his skin—and unhesitatingly gave him as bride the loveliest of his sisters, Princess Sunshine, who from her first sight of the stranger had not been able to take her shining eyes off him.

But no more than a year, the story went, were sun and moon together, for the birth of a girl cost the life of the princess. Hereupon a hundred envious courtiers plotted against the foreigner, since they thought his position was now shaken. He shrewdly unmasked them, but in his gentleness begged for their lives. Then, it is told, one day the caliph's slaves drove ten mules, each laden with a sack, through the gates of the prince's palace. And when his household servants opened the sacks, the heads of the hundred enemies tumbled onto the marble paving of the courtyard. The receiver of the gift grew pale at the sight of the bloody presents, and withdrew to his chambers. When night came, he lifted his child from the cradle, mounted a horse, and left the sleeping city of Cordova. With him, the storyteller concluded, fortune and power turned their backs on the king, forever.

In the fervor of his narration the storyteller swore that he had known Prince Moonlight in person and had often greeted him in the square of Cordova, crossing his arms, humbly, across his chest. He said that their ages were not very different, and that not ten years had passed since those events.

He was convinced that he spoke the truth. But I did not

fully believe him, for the Moors, reverend sir, can lie with more sincerity than we can, because their vivid powers of imagination mislead them into confusing what didn't happen with what did.

Shortly before I left I heard the brown-skinned youth tell the story of Prince Moonlight again and—to give him his due—without any noticeable embellishment or alteration. That impressed me. But I had no time to question him in detail, for by then, like Prince Moonlight, I was quietly preparing to make my way home to Christendom, away from those alien customs and fashions.

I MADE THE journey by sea to England, where I soon succeeded in finding employment with the leading bowmaker of the city of London. He had his workshop on the Thames not far from the Tower of London, and he had many apprentices in his employ. Since his skill was sought by king and nobility, his wealth had grown and he could have been called a respected man except that he was of Saxon blood, like all artisans. Since the Conquest the Saxons are considered inferiors and oppressed in a most unchristian way by their Norman masters."

"Oho!" Sir Burkhard interrupted. "Is that the way for a man to talk who strutted half his life in the retinue of King Henry?"

Hans glanced shrewdly at the canon and replied unhesitatingly: "Sir, passing judgment is like shooting arrows; it all depends on the point of view. Back then, living among the Saxons, I stepped aside and doffed my cap when a troop of Normans galloped past on their armored steeds. Later on, when I myself sat high in the saddle, my honor would not have allowed me to be spoken to by a Saxon otherwise than with bared head. Now, when Saxon and Norman are fading images for me, in the wisdom of my gray hairs, I take a moderate middle position. I say now that power and conquest are ordained by God, and since the Normans have the hotter blood and the fiercer spirit, they are the rulers. But the same God assumed the aspect of a servant and bought us all with His Precious Blood; therefore let the ruler not embitter his servants and not lay hands on his servant's wife and child.

But that is what happened to my master, in whose house, unfortunately for him, a lovely daughter was growing up. Indeed, the golden-haired Hilde was the fairest maiden in London, and I could not keep my eyes off her when she sang her ballads to us after supper, which she did without needing to be coaxed."

Overcome by memories, the graybeard gently rocked his broad, jutting forehead back and forth and murmured, rather off-key:

"In London was Young Beichan born,
 He longed strange countries for to see—"

"What are you getting at, Hans?" cried Sir Burkhard, who did not understand English and was beginning to be ill humored.

The armorer emerged from his dream. Reading in the weary features of his aged listener that this introduction was becoming too long and boring, he spoke to him vigorously: "Do you know, sir, what that ballad that young Hilde sang to us was all about? About the birth of a saint from the womb of a Saracen, that same Saint Thomas whose history I am here to tell you!"

The sudden change of course, as Hans steered his little boat out of the channel of his own life into the current of a greater one, jolted the canon. He straightened up in his chair as quickly and as erectly as his age permitted and exclaimed: "Saracen blood in the veins of Saint Thomas? My dear fellow, are you in your right mind?"

"If you had patiently read the parchment that you say the lady in the convent lent you, you wouldn't be staring at me with such amazement in your eyes. For this very point, I'm willing to wager, is most beautifully elaborated in it. After all, the entire clerical establishment of London took a great interest in the matter and meticulously converted the heathen before they would let her enter upon a Christian marriage. They christened her with the name Grazia, or Grace—*Gnade* in German—because of the signal grace with which the Mother of God had blessed the infidel!

During the bridal night of the Saracen a London nun with the gift of prophecy had a vision: she saw a white lily—that is, a saint—sprouting from the new marriage and growing up to heaven. And it came to pass as the nun had foreseen.

But how much had to happen before the saint grew

from that child of heathendom! Blood and unending misery, the fall of a king and if not the ruin, at least the convulsion of a monarchy!

From here on I will narrate sequentially, as you find fitting, who the parents of Thomas Becket were. I am familiar with the story because it was a favorite of the blonde Hilde, who was still young and innocent and accepted as quite natural the miracle that two people who loved each other should meet across land and sea.

It was many years ago that a merchant from London named Gilbert Becket traveled to the Orient and there was surprised and put into fetters by a prince who was journeying in the desert with his riders and his flocks. The heathen's only daughter took pity on Becket because of his bonds and cut them. Within a year she fled after the Saxon, for she had lost her heart to him. In England they tell the story and sing in their ballads how the noble heathen maiden sought and found her beloved although she had only two English names to guide her to her goal: *London* and *Gilbert*. With them she found her way."

"Listen, Hans," the canon said by way of giving expression to a mounting doubt; "you are riding the fabled winged horse just as skillfully as your brown-skinned friend, the storyteller in Cordova. The only thing that is lacking is for you to swear that you were there on the scene."

The bowman shrugged his shoulders calmly. "No, sir; not I. But my master in London, a precise and matter-of-fact man, often told me how, when he was a young journeyman, he used to run through the streets behind the Saracen girl, and how she stopped every passer-by and asked, 'Gilbert?' She came to be known all over the city because of this, so that finally crowds followed her shouting 'Gilbert' along with her. Some did this because of pity for the beautiful starving woman, who rejected food out of grief, others to ridicule the silly creature who was trying to find one Gilbert from among thousands in London, where the name was a common one. Finally, my master said, the real Gilbert, standing at his window and then crossing his threshold, grasped the heathen by the hand and led her to his hearth.

Whenever my master told this story he never failed to add: 'Vagrant heathen women, Hans, bring nothing good to us Christians. If only that child of the desert had stayed in her tent instead of swimming to our England and here bringing into the world the chancellor, that traitor!'

The chancellor, the world-famous chancellor of England, the king's delight and his wisdom, the admiration and the envy of the Normans, the object of hate and secret terror of the Saxons, was in everyone's mouth at that time. His swiftly rising, resplendent star, the favors and dignities showered upon him as if from an inexhaustible cornucopia, his towers, fortresses, abbeys, his enchanted gardens and boundless forests, his retinue of a hundred and then a thousand knights, the golden harness of his horses and mules, the luxurious tables at his feasts and the endless lines of guests, his exquisite garments and his gleaming gems—all these gave the people of London something to marvel at and talk about from morning to night.

As I worked in the shop I could not shut my ears. They resounded incessantly with talk about the son of the Saxon and the Saracen. I was not surprised that his compatriots slandered him as guilty of every sin; it was the result of political circumstances, since the chancellor was the only Saxon who was at home in the sunlight of royal favor. Even so it is something to think about that it was the fathers who found nothing good in the man whom the sons now kneel before and venerate.

The spiteful rumors described him as a bad son, who loathed the smell of his father's oil vats and bales of merchandise. They said the youth had first entered the service of a sybaritic Norman bishop and had there learned to speak mincingly in French, and thereafter no honest Saxon word had crossed his lips. To blot out his Saxon origin on his father's side he had unscrupulously received his first ordination in holy orders from the hands of that Norman.

Then, becoming rich through his father's death, the stories continued, he went overseas. In Calais, dismissing his loyal Saxon servants, he hired a French retinue, bought fine clothes, and set himself up as a knight. Following an impulse of his mother's heathen blood he traveled through Aquitania and Spain to the Moorish court, they said, and there he enjoyed the favor of the king of Cordova. He was said to have practiced astrology and se-

22

cret lore with philosophers from the Orient. Soon he excelled his teachers, so that after his return he was able to bind King Henry to him unalterably through the attraction of infernal arts.

Sir, the kernel of truth in all this was hard to find. All the greater grew my eager desire to see this living legend with my own eyes. But for a long time I had to be patient, for Thomas Becket was staying on the other side of the Channel in Aquitania, which was part of his queen's dowry, as you know.

Finally the day came. I was in the workshop, carving a bolt. On the street a restlessness began, then a pushing and shoving, a buzz of voices. My fellow workers left their tools and climbed up on stools and benches to look out the windows. Drums and cymbals resounded. Behind the mounted musicians came a herald with the three leopards across his chest, clearing a way for the son of the heathen Grazia.

He was a handsome man, and regal as King Solomon. He could not compete with the Normans in ruddiness of countenance or in size. But he controlled with incomparable bearing his prancing Arabian steed, whose harness was ornamented with gold; and his colorless face had a grave charm.

While I was admiring him, standing as I was among the lowly people, I had no inkling that before long I would enter the service of the king and would there meet this splendid lord every day, indeed almost every hour.

That came about in this way: The Normans came and went in my master's workshop, because there were always crossbows there to be tried out—crossbows with newly invented or perfected devices. Unfortunately the shy Hilde was not always hidden during these visits. She was the joy and desire of my eyes; so it did not escape my notice that the eyes of the Norman knights lingered on her more attentively than was wholesome. There was one of them they called Gui Malherbe—that is, 'Guy the Weed'—who kept his noxious body and soul together in the retinue and at the board of the chancellor. He was a shameless, profligate aristocrat, but he had smooth manners toward women. Every day he vexed and angered me more and more, and it gnawed at my heart to see him dallying with the Saxon maiden on the borderline be-

23

tween veiled flirtation and the brazen arrogance of a nobleman, without my being able to push my knife between his ribs. It might have cost me my life; but chiefly I did not want to cause disaster for my master and the maiden, which such an act would have brought about.

Why should I make a long story of it? Surely Sir Burkhard can remember from his own youth how adroitly the Evil One can spread out his net and then draw it tight in such cases.

One day my master and I had been summoned to a castle some miles from London to install an armory for a Norman lord. It may well have been a planned arrangement. We were delayed on all kinds of pretexts, and when we returned to London young Hilde had disappeared. She had been forcibly carried off, according to the neighbors, who during the night had heard the trampling of horses and cries of distress; the cowardly apprentices and frightened maids lied when the master questioned them and said she had gone willingly.

I suspected Gui Malherbe. What am I saying? Suspected? I was certain! So I advised my master to kneel and block the way of the chancellor when he rode past our workshop on his way to the Tower of London—he had been elevated to the stewardship of the Tower—and not yield until the chancellor gave him a hearing and called his Norman follower to account.

And so it happened one day. My poor master threw himself in the dust before the chancellor's splendidly caparisoned palfrey and tearing at his beard, with choked voice and tear-stained cheeks he demanded justice against his child's abductor, who rode defiantly but with uneasy glances in the third rank behind his almost ostentatiously splendid commander.

I can never forget it. I can see now how the chancellor, serene and unmoved, without a change of expression, barely swept past the stricken man with a glance from half-closed eyes, and slowly guided the horse around him.

The despairing Saxon jumped to his feet and shook his fists and shouted: 'It is too bad, priest, that you don't have a daughter a Norman can ruin for you!' Thomas Becket gently brought his horse to a somewhat quicker gait, as though some bothersome insect was buzzing around him. I forced the old man back into the house to escape the jeering looks and sneering jokes of the troop accompanying the chancellor.

Miserable days followed, that even today I think back on with bitterness; at the time I did not think I would survive them. It was no better when unexpectedly one day poor Hilde sat in the empty workshop at twilight waiting for her father; she knew that at nightfall he locked the shutters and the door with his own hands.

I never found out if Malherbe returned his captive voluntarily because he had gotten tired of her, or if the chancellor in his inconspicuous way had put pressure upon him. One thing I could see clearly: With the best of intentions the master was driving me out of the house. He was resolved to marry his crushed and frightened child to an Anglo-Saxon, a distant relative named Trustan Grimm, who worked in the shop—a coarse-grained uncouth redhead. He did not want me to see that happen. So he kept urging me every day to look for a better job. Meanwhile, to recover from my wretchedness and rage, I had invented a crossbow that carried farther and was easier to crank up than any existing at that time. It was a fine piece of work, though I have surpassed it since then. My master persuaded me to present my invention in person to King Henry, who encouraged the noble arts of missilery and archery. I saw that he had my best interests in mind, and I followed his advice.

Chapter Four

"WHEN I STEPPED for the first time before the king of England in Windsor Castle my heart missed a beat and I trembled all over. He was a man of powerful build and imperious bearing, and his unshadowed blue eyes blazed like two flames. At first he looked at me ill-humoredly. But he quickly understood what was involved, more from the crossbow I handed him than from my hesitant words. He wound up the bow, placed the arrow in it, stepped to the open window, and took aim and shot at a crow perched on the castle weathervane, which was motionless in the dead calm. A ringing laugh, and a smile covered his face as the vane turned and the bird fell fluttering into the gutter.

He tested the string and the trigger again. Then he gave me a satisfied look and praised my work. 'That's skillfully made, my boy. Good, take it to my armory and report to the chief armorer as my body servant. Because you are going to stay with me, German, and you may carry my crossbow on the hunt.'

There was no disputing that, even though my heart was not set upon sampling royal service as the highest stake in the game of life.

While King Henry was still talking to me his third son, the half-grown Prince Richard, came running in with a jubilant cry: 'Father, the Norman stallions are here! Magnificent breed!' And the king let his favorite lead him away.

Now a distinguished, pale man in costly garments rose from a deeply recessed niche where he had been sitting, unnoticed by me, in front of a marble table covered with documents. He stepped to me gracefully and slowly, as if he for his part also wanted to be told about my invention. It was the chancellor. I repeated my explanation with more embarrassment—can you believe it?—than when I spoke to the king. I felt nervous, since he listened attentively and let me tell the whole story, and I had the feeling that my uninterrupted speech echoed much too loud and brash in the vaulted hall.

'Your Grace,' I ended, 'is a scholar and no doubt takes no pleasure in the implements of war?'

He lowered his dark eyes and answered affably: 'I love thought and skill, and I am pleased when understanding triumphs over the fist and when from the distance the weaker strikes and overcomes the stronger.'

With that beautiful and judicious praise of the cross-bow, sir, the chancellor had won me without meaning to. I would have expressed my pleasure at his wisdom with words of gratitude if I could have overcome my awe at his pale and superhumanly intelligent face.

I ENTERED the armory and found the chief armorer, a venerable Norman who towered a head above me. Sir Rollo received me haughtily and disdainfully. But he turned his full attention to my invention, for he was the greatest expert in every kind of weaponry in all England. He muttered something complimentary between his teeth and finally came to the point of approving my idea. Then he asked me about my background, and I told him that I came from close to the Swabian lake. He looked at me with interest showing in his rough wrinkled face.

'Reliable people, the Swabians, and we can use that kind here at the court,' he said. 'If you behave honestly, German, you will find no lack of favor and reward. You are entering the service of a powerful lord.'

He showed me the coats of mail and the helmets of the Conqueror and his son, which were hanging on the walls of the long hall, as the first of an endless series of weapons and pieces of armor. And he began to extol the Norman kings in words of high praise, and recount for me their realms and dominions. 'They are mighty on this side of the sea and beyond it, and what they have grasped they never let go. There is only one thing,' he continued, shaking his head. He ordered me not to touch a rusted arrow that lay on the flagstones below the armor of the second king. 'One thing, the last, has gone awry for them. The powerful monarchs, one and all, had bad deaths. This bolt—God and the Devil only know who shot it—cut short the life of King William Rufus, during a jolly hunt. But what can you expect? Brilliant suns mean bloody sunsets.'

So FROM then on I rode behind my lord and king on the hunt and in battle. I found him to be as he had revealed himself to me on that first day: changeable in mood as April, gruff, impatient, quick to anger, terrible in wrath, but then easy to talk to, genial, so that at the right time you could risk a jest and the great ruler along with his servants would laugh until the tears ran down his cheeks.

But the transition from the stable to the anteroom and finally to the threshold of the royal bedroom, where I was allowed to make my bed like a watchdog—that did not happen in one leap but gradually, stage by stage.

King Henry was a mighty hunter like Nimrod. He loved to chase at full speed on the trail of a stag, leaving his attendants far behind. Then at nightfall he would make do with the first resting place he found, for he was a man of few needs. I was there, staying close behind him on my panting horse, and often the only one with him. Sometimes I had to put him to bed drunk, when after the sweat and exertion of the hunt he had resorted vigorously to the goblet. Thus he got used to having me serve him, and although I didn't ingratiate myself by crafty tricks, still I had enough sense not to do anything foolish to spoil my advantage.

Three things were in my favor: that I was neither Norman nor Saxon; that I accepted no pay or gift from anyone but the king, excepting only rarely and under special circumstances from the chancellor, whom nobody could refuse; and that without exactly pretending to be stupid I acted a little more gullible than I really was, and a little more innocent than experience had made me. Accordingly Sir Henry found satisfaction in my Swabian guile-lessness.

Sir Thomas also helped me to royal favor by looking upon me with good will—for the king saw the world through his chancellor's eyes—and by occasionally direct-ing to me a jesting but meaningful remark which defer-ence would have forbidden his saying directly to King Henry, but which he nevertheless wanted the king to hear.

I gained the chancellor's good will one day when he and I put our fingers to our lips. During the first year of my royal service it happened that Sir Henry had lain down for a nap on a sultry summer afternoon. The chancellor wanted to see him on a matter of urgent business. I went to meet Sir Thomas and whispered, putting my finger to my lips, 'Excellency, the king is asleep.' Now you must know, reverend sir, that the heathens in Granada, of both high and low estate, have the pious habit of adding, whenever sleep is mentioned, 'Praised be He who neither slumbers nor sleeps.' They say this from childhood on and think no more of it than we Swabians do of our 'God send you a good day.' When I lived among the heathens I accus-tomed myself to this saying, in order to fit in with the ways of the country without incurring any sinful guilt.

I don't know whether I myself was drowsy, or if in the semidarkness of the room with the drawn curtains the chancellor, looking even more bloodless than usual, re-minded me of a Moor, or if I just acted from habit. Any-how, I said: 'Excellency, the king is asleep. Praised be He who neither slumbers nor sleeps.'

The chancellor smiled involuntarily until his pearl-white teeth gleamed. Then he asked me in a serious tone: 'How does a German come to use that greeting?'

While we waited for the king to wake up, I told the chancellor that I had studied the art of bowmaking in Granada for three years, and I told him the story of Prince Moonlight. To be sure, this was risky and could have ruined me. But the temptation to determine if Prince Moonlight and the chancellor were one and the same and to test whether that perpetual self-control could be taken by surprise—that temptation was too strong for me. Sir Thomas, though, didn't flicker an eyelash. For a time he kept his eyes lowered, as he was in the habit of doing.

Then he raised them and looked at me, and slowly he put his white finger across his mouth. I bent my knee before him and announced him to the king, whom we heard stirring about in his chamber.

Since both the lords liked me and trusted me, you can believe the surprising fact that I enjoyed the rare privilege of standing behind the throne when the king conferred with the chancellor on affairs of state. King Henry had the sparkling white French wine poured into his goblet while he listened with cunning eyes and inner pleasure as he followed the analyses and complex chess moves of his chancellor, and the latter sunned himself in the radiance of royal favor like a slender white serpent.

King Henry regarded with self-satisfaction the man he had raised from nothing as his creation; but, reverend sir, the creature had become indispensable to the creator and controlled him with his mild will.

I have often stood there while the king's horses, already saddled, were whinnying and stamping in the courtyard. But the chancellor, delaying him just as he was crossing the threshold, would unroll the scrolls and gently force him to listen despite his headstrong impatience. And I had to admire the way he would stand there with a pencil in one hand and parchment in the other, repeating and elaborating the king's casual decision so that the words flowed along like liquid gold."

"Your account, too, flows along in a way that I have to admire," the venerable canon said teasingly.

"Let me tell my story, and let me describe the most amazing man who has trod the earth, the model and the pattern of his century. The highest nobility of England gave their sons as his pages to be trained by him. Any young nobleman who had not been dubbed a knight at the hand of this Saxon parvenu was not considered truly knighted among those arrogant disdainful youths. Those pretty boys, who would never have soiled their lips with an English word, hung on the pale lips of Thomas Becket, who, as a matter of fact, spoke the French of the ruling class more gracefully than any of them. They carefully noted every one of his turns of phrase, they marveled at the neatness of his witticisms, they copied the cut of his clothing, they imitated his serene gestures as the summit of earthly perfection.

But the chancellor lacked one quality, I think: a manly, hot-blooded, quick temper.

Not that he was a coward! No coward could have survived a single day at King Henry's court, for the Normans are more sensitive in points of honor than any other aristocracy. The sword leaps from the scabbard in an instant, and he is a lost man who cannot parry and return the thrust of a blade.

Although he was partly a cleric, Sir Thomas was skilled in the use of weapons and every knightly usage; his supple figure was an advantage for him. When affairs of state permitted, he even went into battle with the king. Once I climbed right at his heels up a scaling ladder and saw him fighting in hand-to-hand combat with a raging Picard inside the city wall we had climbed. He was deathly pale and clenched his teeth as he fought. But he eluded his enemy's weapon and with precise aim plunged his sword through the fighter's heart. Then, when his enemy lay in a pool of his blood, Sir Thomas looked at his sword with loathing and threw it away. 'Bowman, give me a clean one!' he commanded. Yet this sword was a masterpiece of foreign metalworking and cut through the meshes of a coat of mail as though it were cutting through a piece of cloth. I picked it up and used it for years for my protection.

Sir Thomas could not shed blood. Throughout his extensive possessions the animals grazed and played in the clearings as in the Garden of Eden. When he visited the forests the deer came to him and ate from his hand.

He could not sign a death warrant without turning pale. He could not bring himself to witness an execution—a frequent occurrence in an orderly state—whereas my lord the king was pleased to preside at such occasions as the incarnation of justice. King Henry used to laugh at the way his chancellor would look in the other direction when they rode past a place of execution—not because of any spirits that might haunt the place (for the chancellor was a skeptical man), but because of horror at the thought of the tortured human beings whose broken bodies had twitched there on the rack, as he once explained.

The chancellor even refused to sign the sentence of a notorious self-confessed sorceress; and for a heathen whim this otherwise judicious man set himself in opposition to all England—king, peers, commons, and clergy.

That was Black Mary, who carried on her devilish practices in a village not far from London. She brewed thunderstorms, spread plagues, strangled cattle and little children, until at last she was put to the torture in an ecclesiastical court. After she had freely confessed, she had been reprieved to the temporal earthly stake, to save her repentant soul from eternal fire.

Then the pampered chancellor sought out the fiendish creature in her disgusting cell and had her tell him about her forsaken childhood and her later intimacy with the Devil. And can you believe it? Sir Thomas tried to talk Black Mary out of her beliefs about Satan, although she screamed tearfully for the purifying flame. He tried to persuade her that she was deceiving herself and others. And the more vividly she described everything, the more skeptical the heathen became.

Sir Thomas insisted on laying the case before the king. But King Henry refused to consider clemency and declared majestically: 'I cannot; I am England's Christian conscience.' The chancellor replied with composure: 'What can I do against the wisdom of the century which, sire, is your wisdom?' and he signed the warrant.

Later, leaving the room, he turned to me where I was standing by the threshold: 'Mary is no more a witch than I am a saint! Hans, old man, there are moments when I shudder equally at what human beings are and what they imagine they are.'

I didn't understand what he meant, but I had to suspect that Sir Thomas's arrogant philosophy had no room for a belief in Satan's arts.

Later on, when the time came to take Black Mary out to execute her, they found the cell empty. When King Henry threateningly called on the chancellor for an explanation, the latter gave as his opinion that it must have been some kind of magic trickery like everything that had happened before. With that the whole affair was dropped.

There was a report afterward that Black Mary had not departed amid sulphurous fumes but was leading a quiet retired life in a remote dairy farm of the chancellor's. If she had indeed truly repented, let us not begrudge it to her! I am willing to confess to you that I too pitied the poor sinner when I saw her sitting on that pile of mouldy straw looking up at the chancellor with her puzzled black eyes through the tangled strands of her hair and heard her tell sadly about her unsheltered childhood and the wrongs that had been done to her when she was still an inexperienced girl. For I too could tell a story!

You can see, sir, for I have revealed it to you in all honesty, that when the chancellor visited the witch he had me accompany him, as a reliable man."

The canon looked at the bowman, searchingly. "It was you, Hans, who liberated that evil woman?"

"Do you really think so, sir?" Hans answered, and it seemed as if his mouth moved slightly under his beard. Then he steered in another direction.

"A worse witch who lived in England at that time could not be burned at the stake, and for a valid reason: my lord the king was married to her.

Why King Henry had married Eleanor, the divorced wife of the king of France, will be evident to anyone who studies a map and calculates the countries she brought to him: Gascony, Guienne, and Poitou, with countless castles and cities.

In her younger days, they say, she was charming and modest; I will not pluck that spring blossom from her wreath. But at the time when I bent my knee before her she had a dark helmet of exuberant hair, shifty eyes, and feet that were always in motion.

King Henry kept her away from the court: sometimes in an abbey, for she was devout from time to time; sometimes in a remote castle with a few servants, whose number was occasionally increased by an ambitious posthumous son or a knight errant who wanted to associate with a highborn lady.

When the chancellor could not avoid her, he treated her with profound respect, although I believe he found her unattractive, for he loved delicacy and decorum in women. His eye found delight—even though the great false Prophet has forbidden his followers to take pleasure in pictorial representations—in the pure white marble forms of the statues of women which he had installed in his palaces. I doubt whether you have ever seen any. They had been dug out of the ruins of Greek temples, and the

34

emperor of Byzantium had sent several of them to the chancellor in return for a political favor. They are dead stones without power of vision; yet if they are looked at for a time they begin to come to life, and I have often stood in front of those cold creations trying to puzzle out whether they are cheerful or sad.

But the chancellor found nothing pleasant about Queen Eleanor, who was not made of marble; and, for her part, she hated him from the bottom of her heart. It is possible that like the chaste Joseph leaving his scarlet mantle in the hands of Potiphar's wife, the chancellor had once rebuffed her. For although she was orthodox—I have never heard anything against her in this respect—she found something fascinating about heathens. They say that long ago she took a liking to a beardless Saracen when she accompanied her pious first husband on a crusade to the Holy Land.—You must have heard about this, sir, for it was talked about all over the world. Or perhaps she hated him only because he kept a sharp eye on all her doings as a danger and threat to the kingdom. Remember, sir, that her three countries belonged to the princes Henry, Geoffrey, Richard, and John as their maternal inheritance. So the chancellor needed all his skill to hold Queen Eleanor in check, moderately, to assure a reasonable gait—not so loosely that the moods of her hot blood could bring disgrace upon England and the king, and not so tightly that she might rear up in anger and rashly run off with her sons and her lands.

Sir Thomas kept those sons at his side and was a tender father and teacher for them every hour of the day. Inborn character mocks training oftener than it obeys it. Otherwise those four English princes would have been without equals, considering the great love and wisdom the chancellor bestowed on them.

Prince Henry admired only the style of the chancellor's clothes and the distinction of his eloquence, for he was a popinjay and a posturing actor. Prince Geoffrey forgot overnight what yesterday he had loved and sworn by; in his changeable way he could not carry through either sport or serious business. Sir Thomas was especially fond of the king's third son, Richard Lion-Heart, and I became attached to him, too. By nature he was as straightforward as a blast on a hunting horn and as impatient as a young racehorse foaming at the bit. There was no resisting it: you simply had to like the boy! But good sense was not in him, not a penny's worth; and at this moment he is a prisoner in a tower down there in Austria because of one rash act. Prince John, the fourth son—God keep my tongue from speaking against him, for he now stands next to the throne—but a more worthless, malicious brat never trod this earth. This hand of mine often itched to punish him when he gave vent to his malice against me or another one of God's creatures, deliberately damaging one of my finely-wrought crossbows or tormenting a dumb animal. How he would laugh! In my whole life I have never heard viler laughter even in a tavern or a marketplace.

Occasionally the chancellor looked on while I gave the boys lessons in shooting. While they were resting he told them animal fables for pleasure and as a warning—tales that I as a hunter particularly enjoyed. In these stories the birds and animals talked and acted according to their natures—or at least according to the natures that we attribute to them. The Arabs invented this clever game so that they could criticize and ridicule their rulers' faults with impunity under the guise of the actions of animals.

When one of the fabled creatures came to grief in the chancellor's narratives, when Bruno the Bear fell into the ditch with a thud, when Isegrim the Wolf dangled in a trap, or some other mischance of the sort, little John suddenly burst out with his shrill, devilish laugh. I would shrink back, startled, although I was familiar with his character. The chancellor, a friend of intelligence, looked at the child sadly. But he did not betray his revulsion at the boy's deformed inner nature, but rather stooped and gave him more attention than the others. I have heard him sigh, contrary to his normal way of acting, when I had to report another one of Prince John's misdeeds.

In truth the chancellor loved the king's children as if they were his own, and he was ill repaid for it.

NOW I COME to tell you of a secret injustice that can be found in none of the chronicles. But it was the shovel that dug the graves of Sir Thomas and Sir Henry, one after the other." Hans the Armorer mechanically folded his strong old hands, as if they had helped hold that shovel.

Chapter Five

"NOW THAT YOU have some insight into King Henry's household," Hans continued, "you can understand even at this distance that the king found neither peace nor pleasure with Queen Eleanor, and that on his campaigns and royal journeys he had an eye for the daughters of his realms on either side of the sea.

I will not conceal from you that I accompanied him on many rides which, as one who had originally come of age under ecclesiastical discipline, I would rather have abstained from and which occasionally made my confession difficult for me. But bear in mind that the king had few trustworthy people around him; on straight and crooked paths my loyalty protected him from domestic dissension and even poisoning or assassination.

For Queen Eleanor was a jealous fiend, although she herself was by no means faithful to her husband. She bribed such of King Henry's grooms as could be corrupted, so that all his escapades were known to her and she could pursue her rivals murderously. More than one the king found dead or suddenly drooping in his arms. So it was only fair that he should have a dependable servant.

ONE DAY THE king arranged a hunt with only a small retinue, in a distant forest where, I knew, he had previously not been in the habit of hunting. Toward evening a violent thunderstorm overtook us and drove the hunters in all directions. But I stayed close by the king and found a shelter for him under an overhang in a cliff, where he waited out the cloudburst. When the thunder had rolled past and the raindrops were scarcely coming through the foliage of the oaks, I tried to retrace the way we had come. But it was barred by a tangle of fallen branches and shining roots over which the yellow waters of an overflowing brook were rushing. I blew a blast on my hunting horn, but no answer came from any direction. Then the king ordered me to set out toward where the wood seemed thinnest. I did so, and cleared a path for him with my hunting sword. Soon I saw the crimson glow of the sunset glistening on the wet tree trunks. I turned to the king but he pressed past me toward the reddish glow so impatiently that I had trouble keeping up with him.

Then I saw him suddenly check his step, astonished. He stood at the edge of the wood under the dripping foliage and stared motionless toward the setting sun, shading his eyes with his right hand. I stood on tiptoe and craned my neck to look over his shoulder. What I saw seemed like magic or an illusion that would have to dissolve in the next instant.

On a gleaming green forest meadow stood a little castle like some I had seen in Granada. It was surrounded by smooth high walls of yellow stone, and above it rose a little lustrous blue dome. Some slender treetops were visible, trees I would have called cypresses if we had been under a more southerly sky. The delicate but solid structure looked fresh and new and shone like a jewel in the last radiance of daylight.

The king wasted no words. He walked rapidly to the narrow gate and knocked with the hilt of his sword. Nothing stirred inside. Then I too pounded against the wood of the doorway that was sheltered deep inside an arch in the wall. I thought I saw the face of an old man appear in a little window on the side; then it disappeared, and soon after that the bolt was silently drawn back.

A white-haired Saxon opened the door and bowed, silent and trembling, before the king. 'You, Asher?' King Henry said to him and continued, laughing impatiently, 'you certainly aren't going to let your king stand here outside! I'm soaked through and I'm hungry! To whom does this little jewel of a building belong? The chancellor? Or aren't you in his service any more? By Saint George, I have to believe that that austere gentleman has allowed himself to be ensnared by a forest nymph! What Melusine has conjured up all this for his pleasure and relaxation? Quick! Announce me to the charming sprite!'

Now I too recognized the old man and remembered once seeing him trot by our crossbow workshop among the chancellor's followers. At that time he had caught my attention by his melancholy expression and the black eyebrows that met under his white hair. At the court I had not seen him again in Sir Thomas's retinue.

The Saxon looked at the king beseechingly and stammered that it could cost him his life.

'On my oath as a king, it will not. No order that you have been given can apply to me!' King Henry pushed his way in and put his foot over the threshold; he signaled to me to wait outside.

In an extreme of dismay Asher did not know where to turn until my lord ordered him majestically: 'Shut this door and announce to your mistress the visit and favor of her king!'

I sat down to wait, leaning against the wall. I felt comfortable in the cool of the evening, and the rest was welcome. The adventure amused me. I laughed in my beard over Sir Henry's stately last speech. I had to admire the king, considering his hunger and his ripe years, for not appearing before the gate like a singing minstrel but simply announcing to the lady of the castle his dignity and his royal grandeur.

Fool, wretched fool that I was!

AFTER A considerable interval the gate was opened, and King Henry stepped out from the little castle. It was late enough to be pitch dark, although it was the middle of summer. The Saxon led the way for us with a torch along a narrow path which soon brought us to a solitary farm, where we were given horses and a guide.

The dawn was red when we rode in through the gateway of the castle where the king had begun the hunt the day before. As I held the stirrup for him, he gave me a beaming look. He closed my mouth with his left hand and with his right he tossed me a clasp, set with gems, which he ripped off his hat. He had shaken all the gold coins he had in his purse into Asher's hands.

That was the beginning. From Midsummer's Day of

that year until its leaves fell I often accompanied the king through that peaceful forest. Even oftener I made the trip alone, to announce a visit or to bring to his hidden beloved some token of his ardent passion—rare pearls from the sea or the costliest gems yielded by the bosom of the earth. Never did I see her or set foot in the courtyard; I carried out my errands at the gateway, with old Asher. Whenever he caught sight of me he sighed piteously, but he did not refuse obedience nor reject whatever came his way from the royal hand.

I was strictly forbidden to allow myself to be observed on these paths during daylight hours. At all events, they were among the loneliest that I ever traveled. I met no living creature on them, except for a grazing animal and on two occasions, when I was a little late, solitary woodland wanderers.

The moon had waxed and waned since the beginning of this adventure when my brown horse sprained one of his hind legs. I loved the animal like a brother and stayed with him at the farm until I could be sure that I need not worry about him. Then I set out on the return journey on foot, hurrying. It was daylight when I crossed a clearing which was surrounded by deceptive echoes. At the end of the clearing I heard hoofbeats against the rocks. Quickly I threw myself into the bushes and lay flat, watching the long meadow path. There I saw the chancellor's white Arabian, ridden at a slow and relaxed gait. The beautiful animal sniffed delightedly, and through wide open nostrils it breathed in the morning air and the woodsy fragrance.

Sir, I was not surprised to find the chancellor on these green paths. I was prepared to catch sight of him traveling here, sooner or later. The jewel-like stronghold was tended by his servants; the Moorish architecture, the exotic trees in the garden, the unhunted animals round about—all this had long since revealed to me who the builder must be. The king, too, on that first day had guessed who was hiding something precious here.

I don't want to pretend to be better than I am. It delighted me to catch this father of wisdom, this profound scholar, being human; and I had to smile in safe secrecy that it was King Henry, the only one who dared do so with impunity, that had been the encroacher. It has been taken for granted from time immemorial that in amours and affairs of the heart clerics and scholars must yield to princes and warriors.

Naturally I had revealed nothing of my knowledge to King Henry, either by a sly remark or by an amused expression. For there are limits, sir, to the chancy intimacy of a servant with his lord, even the jolliest. In my quiet thoughts I was amused at behavior which I took for a bit of royal mischievousness; but I was becoming entangled in a folly and a horror that cost King Henry his crown, his life, and—alas—the salvation of his soul.

Understand, sir, that I thought the chancellor had taken a vine bearing ripe sweet grapes and transplanted it from some Aquitanian vineyard to the mists of England; and if he should discover some rotted berries on it he would push it to one side indifferently or at most, fastidious as he was, with some disgust. I could imagine how, finding his king and creator as a rival, he would withdraw from the lists with a polite, faintly disdainful expression. Hence I saw in the treachery little wickedness and no danger.

With malicious curiosity I saw from my hiding place the rider slowly go past. A few days earlier he had returned from Canterbury, where the king's priests had caused him some trouble. Now he had been spending his nights in Windsor Castle taking care of matters that had been unattended to during his absence. He wrote indefatigably by the soft light of a Greek hanging lamp so that the king, should he wake from a restless sleep, could look over across the courtyard and see the one who was caring for his interests and those of his kingdom.

But is it the chancellor? Is this the reserved man with the cool appraising glance for the cares of state, I asked myself, or a devout pilgrim and knight questing for the Holy Grail? (You know the story of the chalice with the precious blood that descended on Montsalvatsch amid sweet music from on high?) There rested upon those pale dreamy features a look of blissful purity, and his face shone like moon and stars. His long violet silk cloak hung in priestly folds over the shoulder of the silvery palfrey, which, accustomed to prance to the clash of cymbals and drums, today slowly trod along the soft path, lifting its dainty feet as if to the music of flutes played by hidden forest deities.

I was shocked at the devoutness with which this hypocrite was riding to a sinful assignation—quite differently from my royally audacious master, thirsty for love. And yet I was overcome with sympathy for this betrayed devotion, and then a sudden fear that the pale man there, whose character had always inspired an uncommon awe in me, might take revenge for the plundering of his shrine on us, the king and me, secretly, but with unheard-of cruelty.

At this instant the deep vertical fold of the statesman appeared again between the chancellor's eyebrows. Sir Thomas urged his horse forward, seized not by impatience but by a mounting uneasiness.

ONCE AGAIN the new moon was a crescent in the sky when I was overtaken by daylight on those paths. About midnight the king had taken leave of his mistress because his journey to Normandy was imminent. But then, when we reached the edge of the forest, he sent me back with the message that he wanted to embrace her once more and would return the following day.

After I had carried out this errand I was riding back through the autumnal mists. I was tired and sleepy. My horse brushed the yellow leaves from the branches. I thought gloomily about the transitory nature of earthly existence, as I often did when I contemplated the faint light of the eternal stars.

A loud whinnying quite close by wakened me from my vagrant thoughts. Beyond a turn in the path I saw a saddled nag that was tied to the fence of the farm. I slid off my horse, led it to a thicket, crept back silently, and peered over the fence. Inside the enclosure, discussing something with the suspicious farmer, was a lean fellow in armor. At first his back was turned toward me. Then in the middle of the conversation he turned his head in the direction of the little castle and revealed the sharp beak of a bird of prey. I recognized the vulture, went back to my horse, and galloped off. For my king's pleasure retreat was being spied on by none other than the Norman Malherbe, whom I had hated since Hilde's abduction more than that soldier in the painting of the Passion play on All Hallows' Day—the one who is spitting in the face of our Lord and Savior; I have especially detested him since I was a child. The chancellor had dismissed the vile scoundrel from his retinue, and it was said that he had taken service with Queen Eleanor and found favor with her.

I saw what was in store. If the queen discovered the hiding place of the forest elf, I would not bet a penny on her fragile life.

When I reported this alarming news to the king, the blood climbed dark red into his face, for anger and love. 'We must take the lady overseas,' he said, and frowned. 'And at once! Before the hawk tears the dove to pieces!' He ordered me to have ready that evening three saddled horses and some inconspicuous clothing for him.

IT WAS ALREADY dark. The chancellor had not let the king go until quite late. Sir Henry snatched cloak and cape and leapt on his horse.

After an hour of hard riding we were about half way there. He motioned me to come to his side and told me that I would not go back with him in the morning but was to stay the next day in the little castle and bring the lady after nightfall to the nearest royal castle, from where he would have her escorted across the sea.

We reached our destination not long after that. The king found a soft pillow for his head, and I had a hard one at the base of the wall—the saddle of my horse, to whom and the two others I granted a night of grazing.

When the foggy treetops were gilded by the rising sun and I had just caught the three horses, the king came out the door. On his arm was a charming creature, not more than fifteen years old. The loveliest girl's head I ever saw leaned on the king's shoulder, and she gazed with two beseeching, frightened eyes into his, which were drunk with love. Coal-black hair, bound with a gold fillet, fell unbraided over her delicate shoulders and hips almost to the ground. She was in tears, and Sir Henry tried to encourage her.

'I am leaving this man here. He is a faithful servant and will guard you as the apple of his eye. This evening, without fear, let him put you on a horse. It has to be so; it is what I want, Grace. Just a little while, and we are united again under a warm sky.'

He kissed her, jumped into the saddle, and galloped away. The girl waved farewells after him with both arms.

But the blood had gone out of me. The truth pierced me like a sharp arrow. Understand this, sir! The king had not supplanted the chancellor as the lover of a splendid ambitious beauty; he had laid hands on Thomas Becket's innocent daughter! For Grace, as the king had called her, was the living image of the chancellor, in so far as an innocent young face can resemble one that is coldly calculating and experienced in the ways of the world. The noble line of the forehead, the dark melancholy eyes, the serious smile, the gentleness of the gestures—there could be no doubt: Grace, too young to be the chancellor's sister, was his own flesh and blood. Sir Henry, a Christian king, had sinned worse than any heathen against a child and a scarcely grown body.

Although I was only a poor servant, I was furious at my lord. I clenched my fists as though it was my own child that had been destroyed. At the same time a great sense of sadness came over me, and I could have wept bloody tears. For my king, of whom I was deeply fond, had provoked the wrath of God by his murder of innocence. I tried to find excuses for my exalted master in his hot blood, his complete power, the acts of his blind and thoughtless hours. But in vain! It kept ringing in my ears: Your lord has committed a mortal sin! My senses were unsealed, and I saw Grace's guardian angel holding a white cloth before his face, in distress and shame; I heard the trumpets of Judgment Day resounding mightily.

But I pulled myself together. The two animals I was standing between were becoming restless. I held them more firmly and my preoccupied confusion began to fade.

The chancellor's child had disappeared into the castle. Asher stood alone in the doorway and beckoned me for the first time into his little watchman's room, which was built into the thick outer wall.

He looked frightened and miserable and was so absent-minded that he forgot to bring me anything to eat and drink, which I truly needed after my fright. While I got some bread and fetched the wine jug out of the cupboard for myself, he confessed hesitantly that the flight of the beautiful Grace, which the king had ordered, would not be without danger. He admitted that he had reported to his master, the chancellor, in all good faith and honesty, that the Norman Malherbe had been spying on the forest castle and riding around it for several days. Any hour now, he said, he expected the chancellor, who would come with armed men and place a garrison behind the walls.

'If only I had resisted the Evil One,' he moaned in pitiful remorse, 'and had revealed to my lord that first visit of yours! My body would have perished; but now I have sold my soul! But where could I have found the courage to resist the highest authority? Terror and confusion accompany your king. Cursed be the hour of my birth! Those Normans have stolen everything from us, even the knowledge of good and evil. But my lord, the chancellor is also to blame,' he went on. 'He, the embodiment of wisdom, he has educated Grace badly. Will you believe it, Bowman? We have here in the house no crucifix, no missal, no saint's statue, except for a tiny Saint Joseph there in a niche for us servants. He would bring the child parchments covered with Arabic writing, heathen tales which falsify the hard cruel ways of this world into a sweet adventure; and the child found pleasure day and night in that beautified deception and delusion. Even Monna Lisa, the Spanish lute player and her maid, has often in her thoughts found fault with the chancellor because of this. That poor woman! On her knees she tried to bar the king's way. But he filled her hands and pushed her aside. For women your master is irresistible, as he is a cruel king for us. And thus the folly came to pass.'

While the aged Saxon was lamenting, timidly and unprofitably, I had been fortifying myself with food and drink, and my spirits were gradually reviving. 'Hans,' I told myself, 'don't be an old woman. Pull yourself together. A disaster has occurred; but there is still a possibility that things may yet turn out better. Who knows whether Queen Eleanor may leave us—before her time in death or after her time with some passerby? Either way the king would be free and could make Grace his queen. After all she is of princely blood twice over! Worry about today's problems and get that child overseas!'

You must recognize, sir, that I was saying that to cheer

myself. But believe me, I would have given all the possessions I had gained in royal service, my skill, and half my
blood, if I could have ransomed King Henry from his act
and myself from his service. The sin weighed so heavily
in God's balance that its weight could well crush both
master and servant.

Sir Henry had abused the credulity of a child. Grace was
of heathen blood from both parents, and the submissive
Arab women bow down to the dust before a scepter. For
them a king represents God and the law, and more than
father and mother. I could understand how Grace could
keep silent to her father about the evil secret of the king.

How ardently and recklessly the chancellor must have
loved his daughter if he, who in everything else kept close
watch on all sides and espied all developments of a situation, kept her near him and hence near the Norman
court—thus I brooded—and how grievously he will
regret it!

But quickly I collected myself to attend to what needed
to be done. I took three round loaves of bread under my
arm and led my two horses, which were tied outside, into
a nearby ravine with a clear brook, fed them and let them
drink, and fastened their bridles to two fir trees. I was glad
to care for two intelligent and loyal animals who knew
nothing about treachery and sin.

As I was coming out of the ravine I was startled by a
bugle call which came from another corner of the forest
and was answered by the waving of a cloth from the battlement around the blue dome. Hurriedly I crossed the
space separating me from the castle wall. In the shadow of
the wall I slunk to the gate; the pale trembling Asher
drew me in.

His little gatekeeper's room had three narrow peep-
holes, giving views to the outside, the gateway, and the
castle courtyard.

About a dozen riders galloped out of the wood. The
chancellor was in the lead; I recognized him by his slender gray-white Arabian and the serious way he was riding
it. He was in full armor with lowered visor. In front of the
gate, where they dismounted, he ordered some of the
knights to take the horses off in the direction of the farm.
The others followed him through the gate—a sight that
was by no means to my liking. In the courtyard they re-

ceived orders to take their positions on the battlements.

I had shifted to another peephole to keep the chancellor in sight. Asher seemed to be giving him an account; then he vanished into the living quarters of the castle. The old watchman wore the key to my hiding place at his belt. I was entrapped, and I could only keep hidden and wait.

Right across from me, in the center of the courtyard, was the dome structure, surrounded by a semicircle of terraces covered with luxuriant evergreen bushes. After a while Sir Thomas came through the high vaulted door, leading Grace by the hand. They sat down on a gleaming marble bench beside a basin with reddish streaks, above which jets of water shot up and intersected. I was looking at the chancellor's serious but unsuspecting expression and Grace's enigmatic little face. I was so close that I suddenly ducked my head, although the outside of the wall that I was peeping through was overgrown with ivy.

Now the chancellor waved aside the maid who was standing, with lowered eyes, in the doorway—probably that Spanish Monna Lisa whose virtues I had just been hearing about from Asher. For a time they sat in silence, and Grace looked at the sparkling water to avoid her father's eyes.

THEN THE chancellor began, in Arabic: 'My child, you will stay here for a few more days. It is possible that you will be alarmed by a raid. But don't be afraid. I am leaving here for you ten valiant fighting men who are entirely capable of holding these walls against a surprise attack. You must get used to the sound of weapons, my timid little dove. That is the lot of every mistress of a castle in these unpredictable and crimeridden days.

'And the time has come, my dear one, when I must part from you and give you in marriage. Of course not under these damp skies, but beyond the sea in a sunny land with gentler customs—when it is possible and your star leads you there, not far from your foster parents in Poitou. Surely you still remember the honest Calas, of whom they say that he is of Moorish descent, just because he speaks Arabic, although he says his Our Father just as we do? After all it is scarcely a year since the old man brought you here and parted from you with tears.

'I do not know whether it was a good thing,' he said, and

furrows appeared on his forehead. Since Grace said nothing, he continued as if excusing himself: 'But shouldn't I for one short interval in my life rejoice in having your innocent youth to myself? But now the time that I could allow myself has passed, and the moment of separation has come. I dare not endanger this beloved head!' And he laid his narrow hand on her hair.

'The king is traveling to the Continent tomorrow, and I am to follow in a few days. You will accompany me, heavily veiled, with your women; and you will not stir from my side until I give you into the care of a brave and excellent man.

'Some time when the king is drunk with his unclean pleasures he will allow me one day for my pure joy. This king!' he said contemptuously as if he saw him there in person. I was truly amazed to hear him speak that way.

'Do not fear,' he went on, for the hand that he held twitched in his; 'I know how to choose. I will be watchful about the one I betroth you to, and even from afar I will hold my protecting hand over you, for I have power in all Norman lands.

'And you do not want to close the doors of a nunnery behind you, do you? No; your eyes tell me: you have no sin to atone for; you need light and sun.'

If the wise Sir Thomas had not been so preoccupied with his own thoughts he would have been aware of the agony of his child; but his eyes were bandaged.

Grace struggled for words, and finally she whispered faintly: 'Who is it, father, who is a danger to me here?'

'Who?' the chancellor repeated, with a quaver in his voice. And as if he had resolved to conceal the wickedness of the world from his child no longer, he said without evasion: 'A befouled queen. She hates me. Her spies have informed her of your existence. I do not want Queen Eleanor to know about you and plot against you—her very thoughts defile.' Grace grew pale; I realized that Sir Henry had judiciously not spoken to her of his wife, who was nothing to be proud of.

She gathered her strength and said softly: 'You have not always spoken so, my lord and father. Hadn't you decided to introduce me some day before the face of the king? Haven't you extolled his favor as that of a kindly and majestic master? And you have praised Prince Richard to me.'

'If I talked that way,' Sir Thomas replied gravely, 'I spoke foolishly and I must have been led astray by my fatherly pleasure in you. I have better plans; let that idle talk drift away like the air in which its echoes died. You must not go to the court, into that pestilential atmosphere where nothing pure can thrive. But in one matter what you say is the truth: the king deserves reverence and obedience.

'But enough! My hour is done. Entrust yourself to my care as my child, and with no further thought. You know that I love only you, don't you? Beyond measure!' And he kissed her gently on the forehead.

Sir Thomas stood up. He looked around searchingly, to make sure that each of his soldiers was keeping watch on the battlement assigned to him. His glances were so sharp and penetrating that even in my dark hiding place I slid down to the floor and only heard the words: 'In three days, then. Be ready. Good-bye until then.' And an order to the commander of the ten: 'You will let no one in or out, on peril of your own life.'

WHEN I STOOD up again, the marble bench was empty. Thomas Becket and his unfortunate daughter had disappeared.

I shuddered to see for the first time the man I thought of as omniscient deceived and betrayed. It filled me with horror that a father's faith in the precious innocence of his child had been used by the Devil to bedazzle the sharp eye of the wisest of men and drive a poisoned arrow through the most complete armor.

After a while the chancellor's Arabian mare was brought, Sir Thomas rode off, and the key grated in the door of my little room. Asher stared at me with hopeless dull eyes. I saw that he was entirely helpless; so I took control.

'Go across there,' I said, 'and take to Monna Lisa, the lute player, an order in the name of the king, to prepare her mistress for travel and to be at the gateway tonight when your lamp is extinguished. Go!'

He came back with the answer: she would follow the

instructions. I ordered him to light his lamp as soon as it began to get dark and sit at his slate with chalk in hand, just in case one of the sentries marching back and forth on the battlement across the courtyard should look suspiciously at the lighted window. I lay down on his bed in a corner, since I needed rest after the strain of the day. But the groaning old man kept disturbing me with his worried murmuring and his monotonous self-reproach. I told him to be quiet, but still I couldn't sleep.

It is cruel how the thoughts continue on their way, tirelessly and independently, when the heart is oppressed by anxiety. My thoughts went round and round, working on the question why the chancellor had to give his unfortunate child the name Grace. Perhaps it was in honor of his mother, who had been christened so. Perhaps he had yielded to a heathenish impulse, for Grace signifies heavenly mercy—which may God grant all of us!—but also the most delicate flowering of human qualities and human charm.

Another thing fed my thoughts: Sir Thomas had told Grace about Richard, his favorite. In doing so possibly he had indulged in the wicked ambition of taking his child to King Henry's court and bringing her to princely honors.

I went to sleep thinking about this, and the god of dreams beguiled me with all sorts of tricks. It is well known, of course, that sadness in dreams signifies joy, and happy dreams mean tears. It seemed to me that once again I was coming out of the forest behind King Henry, when his face suddenly was transformed into that of a young man and became Richard's. The headstrong prince knocked at the gate of the forest castle and smashed the door with one blow of his armed fist. The loyal Asher boldly threw himself in Richard's path, and Monna Lisa's virtuous tears protested angrily.

But see! There, out of the inner part of the castle, comes the chancellor, leading Grace by the hand. He grasps Richard's right hand and leads the two under the arching trees. But this is transformed into the vaulted ceiling of the hall at Windsor. The bridal couple, radiant in beauty, kneel before Henry and Eleanor, who look on them with parental satisfaction. Drums crash, trumpets blare. I throw my felt cap in the air and shout: 'Long live Prince Richard and Princess Grace!'

Then I woke up and heard the sallow sinner Asher murmuring prayers. Stepping to the window I caught sight of the light in the castle apartment where Monna Lisa and the immature mistress of an old king were waiting for my lamp to be extinguished.

It was a bad night, the worst of my life. Long black clouds were moving across the sky, hiding the waxing sickle of the moon with their trailing garments. The footsteps of the sentry on the battlement had just faded away when I put out the lamp.

'We have two horses, Asher,' I said; 'you will put Monna Lisa on yours.' We groped our way down the spiral staircase. In the gate stood two cloaked women. One of them, the slender one, heavily veiled, was shaken by sobs. I carefully pulled back the bolt and crept through the gateway and peered around and above me. I thought I heard the string of a bow being tightened up there on the wall, but nothing moved—I must have been mistaken.

I waited for as long as it took to say Our Father three times. I never prayed more fervently in my life. A hound howled, then everything was quiet again.

Now I took the trembling Grace, lifted her in my arms, and ran toward the wood as fast as I could. All at once it grew lighter around us; a cloud was driven by the wind so swiftly that the moon rolled out for a moment from behind its cover.

A whistle, a whizzing flight! Would that the arrow had hit me! The slight creature in my arms convulsively seized me around the neck. Warm blood flowed over me. My cheek was scratched by the projecting point of the arrow that had pierced the throat of the chancellor's child. A strangled gasp, and all was over for Grace.

I put the young corpse into the arms of Monna Lisa, who was following at my heels. That irresponsible woman screamed penetratingly. As I reached the wood, arrows were buzzing around me. Asher's gasping breath was following close behind me.

I jumped on one horse, Asher on the other. We raced through the nocturnal forest paths. Asher wavered in the saddle. He and I both bent our heads down into the horses' manes so as not to be swept off by the branches which hung down, lower than usual and black as if they were in mourning.

We reached the big moonlit clearing. The way went downhill from here. Our frightened horses flew along. Then behind me I hear a hoarse yell; I turn and see Asher's black horse, normally a quiet animal, rear bolt upright with bristling mane and suddenly fall over backwards. Something white flashing by had startled him; it could have been one of those white does that Sir Thomas protected in his forest sanctuaries. The horse rolled over beside a pile of field stones, and there lay a dead man with distorted features. My hair stood on end. I spurred my mount forward without looking around again at the dying black horse or the unfaithful servant on whom judgment had been passed.

Chapter Six

"I WENT DIRECT to Dover, to follow King Henry to Normandy. Contrary winds had delayed him, and I found him there. Sooner than I had expected, and still on English soil, the hour had come to report the catastrophe to him.

He broke out in tears of real misery and locked himself in his room. I lay down on my king's threshold as I had long been doing in times of danger. Inside he could not sleep, and all night I heard him pacing back and forth with heavy steps. From time to time he lamented aloud and spoke to himself so violently that I could clearly understand what he was saying amid the sighs.

'She was my delight!' he mourned. 'I would have taken my tender lamb to a safe pasture. But what can I do against the evil character of my queen and the stupidity of my servants? Against the malice of fate? Misery has come from that forest glade for me and the chancellor, both of us.

'But I will write to him what is in my heart. He must be told that I will pour over him my goodwill and favors, more than ever before, and he will forever be nearest to my heart and my throne.'

Toward morning he became calmer. In the first light of dawn he put in place the table and a chair and apparently was writing a letter, murmuring each sentence to himself before he wrote it down. Finally I heard the sound of the heavy impression of his seal.

He summoned me and gave me what he had written.

'You must put this in the chancellor's own hands,' he said. 'Hunt for him until you find him.'

WITH MATTERS in this state the king traveled overseas and I to London with my letter—and that was no light burden, you can believe me. Although I had acted in obedience to my lord, my conscience was sorely oppressed, and I was awed and afraid to appear before the chancellor. For by now he must have brought to light the true circumstances of Grace's destruction.

He was not in London, where I looked first. His city servants could not or would not say in which of his castles he was. I did not need to be told. I knew.

On a fresh horse I raced along in broad daylight—what was there to hide now?—along the same paths which I had ridden so often in dusk and moonlight. A brilliant sky gleamed on the yellow crowns of the trees and between the boughs that had already lost many of their leaves.

My heart pounded like a hammer when I caught sight of the glistening little castle. I jumped from my horse and found the gate, formerly so well locked, standing open. No gatekeeper asked what my business was.

It was quiet in the courtyard; only the wind whispered in the evergreen boughs of the exotic trees, and the fountain played with its golden spheres. I checked my step and looked around for some living creature. Then I observed a woman kneeling before a shrine in the garden wall. She did not notice my coming until I touched her firmly on the shoulder. Monna Lisa turned, frightened, and stared at me with eyes red from weeping. Then she signaled with both hands that I should leave at once. I showed her the letter, and as the king's messenger I demanded to be taken at once to the chancellor.

Trembling but without arguing she climbed the steps ahead of me to the yellow pillars of the dome structure. She opened the door. 'She is lying in the chapel. I have dressed her like a queen,' she said timidly, and vanished.

I stepped into the bright area of a little round hall lighted from above. Around the wall ran a costly cushion, and in the middle there was a gilded cage full of fluttering and twittering. Bright-hued foreign birds were playing there under dwarf palms, but nowhere was there a human being to enjoy this.

I walked across the colored designs of the mosaic floor toward a narrow marble stair which led to a curved door. I opened this and cautiously pushed back the damask curtain hanging over it. There a sight met me that banished words from my lips and shut off my breath. I looked into the half-light of the castle chapel. But there was no crucifix there, no sanctuary lamp with its perpetual light, no body of a saint or a martyr buried under the altar. Instead, the dead Grace lay in front of it, in a casket as richly adorned as the altar itself. A shaft of light poured down from the one window high in the wall. It lighted her more-than-earthly beauty. Her head rested on a purple cushion and wore a coronet of flashing jewels. The tender body was concealed in the folds of a robe, stiff with gold embroidery and pearls, that extended over the edges of the casket. Her clear little hands lay across her breast and held together in a maidenly gesture the black veil of her hair, which framed her head and cheeks, covering the two wounds in her neck and meeting again under the pale marble cross of her arms.

Next to the lovely dead face lay another, bathed in the same beam of sunlight, more faded and lifeless than that of the corpse. It was a face on which the miseries of death and despair had rested and then, their work done, had passed on. The chancellor, his hair uncombed and his clothes torn, lay there beside the casket, resting his arms on its rim.

The silence was almost complete. There was only a whisper of leaves at the window; faint shadows of flowers danced across the purple cushion and the two faces.

I don't know how it happened that in this terrible hour the Moorish customs in Granada came into my mind. I simply tell you the way things happened: Whatever it may have been—the whispered inspiration of a spirit of light or of darkness—I was moved to pronounce in Arabic a verse of the Koran. May God not hold it against me! It may have been that the sight of the pale Grace reminded me of the infidels' paradise and its angels. The heathen saying goes: 'Beautiful they are, and lovely. Yea, they are beautiful as lilies and hyacinths. They close their eyes, and their pure faces have the hue of the ostrich egg that lies well sheltered in the sand.'

This saying had scarcely passed my lips when a change

came over the chancellor's face. An emotion of joy and love glided across it. Slowly he turned to see who had consoled him with this verse from the Koran. I made use of the moment: I approached him, bowed before him, and in profound fear I handed him the royal letter.

It took a while for him to find his way from his entrancement back to this world. But then he caught sight of the three leopards of the royal seal. The hand into which I had put the document jerked back as if stung by a scorpion. He hurled the letter away with an expression of intense pain. Like a man lying on the rack and suffering unspeakably, he contracted his eyebrows. The reproachful eyes were aimed at me. Deep within them a flame smoldered, cruel and angry as the fires of hell. That look struck me with the force of a javelin; dread penetrated to the depths of my being, and I fled without a word of leave-taking.

Chapter Seven

"NOW, SIR, you can feel the horror, and you may suppose that the enmity between the king and Thomas Becket broke out at this time. You would be mistaken. For a while they shunned each other's company; but there was a good reason for this and it happened naturally, since King Henry was on the other side of the sea warring against the Capetians, and in the meantime the chancellor was attending to affairs in England.

My lord's faith in the chancellor's wisdom and loyalty was unwavering; this trust could not be shaken. And for his part Sir Thomas never more willingly took on himself every burden of work and partisan hostility that his zeal for the greatness of his king required of him.

At that time his position was not an easy one. To promote the royal rights he had become embroiled in an obstinate quarrel with the aristocratic Norman clergy. You know about such disputes, sir, because they are rampant everywhere. In England they grew out of the excessive privileges the Conqueror had attached to the episcopal sees. Not only were all legal proceedings between priest and priest exempted from the royal law courts, as in other countries, but also any layman with a case against a priest had to cite his tonsured adversary in an ecclesiastical court. Since—to put it bluntly—no crow pecks out another crow's eyes, clerics committed murder and rape (not to mention minor crimes) and went unpunished. Or, even worse, they were punished so mildly that it was a bad joke, and the unquenched passions of the tonsured ones grew and grew.

This infuriated my lord and king, for in ordinary matters he was a just man. He tried to restrain his clergy. No easy task!

For reasons of state the Conqueror had completely subordinated all the other bishoprics of England to that of Canterbury. At this time a defiant Norman was sitting on the throne of the primate and archbishop of Canterbury. He made good use of his tonsure to raise his banner against his liege lord and monarch. And the Holy Father in Rome at that time—it was said that he had been hauled out of a monastery and put on the papal throne—had in his whole life had little experience or comprehension of the world and its affairs. He took the side of the Norman bishop because he did not want any ecclesiastical privilege of any kind to be lost. The chancellor of England sent many official documents to this pope, appealing to the deaf ear of His Holiness, requesting him to impose rules and set limitations on this degenerate ecclesiastical law system.

I can say to you, sir, for I know on which side the canons of Saints Felix and Regula take their stand, that nothing more equitable or subtle has ever been written or will be written against the secular power of priests than the documents that flowed from the chancellor's versatile pen. He did not damage his case with insulting comment or longwinded preachments; that accomplishes nothing in diplomatic dealings. He assailed the simple mind of the Holy Father with striking facts. He broke open one window shutter after another, so to say, so that bright daylight could enter and even a child had to understand: avarice, covetousness, robbery, treachery, lechery, deeds of violence such as King Henry's clergy was guilty of were something very different from the pure blameless behavior of the Savior and his twelve apostles.

Perhaps it was only to conquer his grief. At all events, the chancellor struggled manfully. He enlisted Scripture, church fathers, legal experts in his cause; and his sharpest sword was the gospel text: 'My kingdom is not of this world.'

On your lips I see the question how I could have known these things. Hear me. Whenever a message or an official letter of the chancellor arrived at the camp for the king's signature—for the chancellor contended with the pope in the name of the king—if none of the king's clerics happened to be available, he had his unworthy servant read the correspondence aloud. He knew that I had followed a priestly path in my youth and knew how to read, whereas his own eyes, however sharply and surely they could see in the distance, had become unfit for deciphering handwriting.

He laughed heartily at the striking likenesses of his clergy that the chancellor was drawing. 'Notice, Hans,' he would say to me, 'he takes delight in dragging my priests around by the hair. He is an unbelieving philosopher and a disguised Saracen.'

I, too, often had to smile, but hardly with any happiness. Not that I would begrudge a pope as such that kind of treatment, in view of the character of some who from time to time happen to hold the title of Holy Father. But there seemed to me to be something that my lord was missing entirely in his somewhat simple-minded way: under this dextrous wit an abyss of reproving seriousness and deep sadness was burning.

Sir, I could not forget that face in the castle chapel.

Often while I was carving an arrow and gave my thoughts free rein I wondered if Sir Thomas would ever be able to sit at the royal table again and exchange jokes with King Henry and breathe the same air with him. The king seemed to have no doubt of it; with his inborn sturdiness he put past things behind him.

But in my mind I wagered against him. The judgment in my heart was that it ran counter to human possibility.

AFTER THE WAR was over the king was staying at one of his strongholds in Normandy. One day, having nothing to do for a change, I went up to the tower and chatted with the watchman there. He gave me his post for a while, since his girl friend had beckoned to him from the kitchen garden.

As I kept watch I caught sight of a troop following the twists of a road leading down a little hill. A rider in armor was in the lead, shining in the evening sun; he blew a blast on a hunting horn. It was Lion-Heart! Behind him rode his three brothers and a retinue of knights. Now I

59

catch sight of something white and shiny—the chancellor's horse. A laugh of scornful confidence comes over me. I grasp the watchman's big horn, reply to Prince Richard's call, and greet the chancellor impudently—admittedly the words were in my ordinary speaking voice and of course unintelligible at that distance: 'Sir Thomas, you have no real marrow in your bones and no knightly blood in your veins. *A la bonne heure*—a fine thing, this! It will be all right with me if my king decides to roast you alive and make a Saint Lawrence out of you!' When I caught sight of that white horse I decided that master and servant no longer had anything to fear and that Heaven would have no part in a cowardly man's revenge. I hurried down and watched the entry, keeping as much to one side as possible.

Sir Thomas had not changed. His gestures were as calm and his clothes as elegant as before. The king, in his impetuous way, rushed to his sons and his chancellor, whom he had probably longed for more than for his children. The chancellor spared him any occasion for a show of shame or regret; he bowed respectfully and then spoke of the boys with solicitude and benevolence. However, he added mildly and quietly, the demands on his time, the increasing cares of state, his travels and missions, and also a weariness he had never felt before, would no longer permit him to guide their education himself. He would select eminent men as their tutors, who could easily make him unnecessary.

The king stood there, taken aback by this statement, and his sons surrounded the chancellor tearfully, begging him not to leave them. Only little Prince John made a grimace of pleasure. The king joined the boys in asking him not to deny himself to them.

The chancellor's eloquent lips repeated his refusal with new graceful turns of phrase; but his dark eyes were turned toward the king and seemed to say: 'Cruel man! You have stolen my child and now you ask me to concern myself with yours.'

I do not know whether King Henry read the message in that look, but he stopped urging the chancellor.

FROM THAT hour strife broke out among the four princes. The chancellor's love was not there to bring them to reconciliation, for he had become indifferent about them and abandoned them to their impulses.

I have already told you that I was the princes' teacher of archery and the use of the crossbow. I was strictly forbidden to leave them alone or to leave any of them with a crossbow in his hands. Since they were of unlike and unbrotherly natures, care had to be taken to prevent their attacking one another with a weapon.

One day I was carrying four crossbows to the princes in the rear courtyard. Amid the barking of hounds I heard loud noises and yells of fighting. I found the boys so entangled that I had a hard time separating them. Lion-Heart had Prince Geoffrey by the throat with his right hand and with his left he held Prince Henry by his curly hair; and he was shaking both of them thoroughly. Little Prince John was on the side of the two older ones; he was clawing at Richard's back, and bit him in the neck. First I pulled the little wildcat away and then released Henry and Geoffrey from Lion-Heart's fists.

Prince Richard turned on me in flaming anger and shouted: 'In the name of the Devil, Bowman, do you want to steal our birthright from us?' 'What birthright, beausire?' I asked, startled. 'To hate each other,' he yelled. 'We won't renounce that right!'

I felt a deep pity at these words from a youngster. I took him aside and gave him a Christian talk on the sweetness of brothers dwelling together in harmony. But Prince Richard broke out in violent weeping and sobbed: 'He didn't even look at me today!' I guessed that he was referring to Sir Thomas. 'If the chancellor is spending less time with you,' I said to comfort him, 'it is due to the weight of official business for the advantage of your father, whom he loves.' Prince Richard shook his head stubbornly. His blue eyes flashed at me, and he shouted: 'You're telling a lie, Bowman! The chancellor does not love my father!'

The four not only fought with each other. Alas, they began to fail to show proper respect for their father's majesty. I still remember how it pained me once to have to look on and listen when I accompanied the king to his bedchamber. He had wearied his head with official business and his body in a stag hunt. His head was bent over his nightcap drink; he had laid it on his arms on the table, and was snoring.

In the corridor we had met the two worst ones of his sons, the oldest and the youngest. If the king had been fully in possession of his senses, little Prince John would have bowed and scraped before him, but now he impudently walked behind the royal steps, staggering as if he was drunk. And the other, that clotheshorse, turned away from his begetter with an insolent 'Disgusting!'

After I had cared for my lord, I met Prince Henry in the corridor. I scolded him roundly, told him he was like Noah's son, the black Ham; I threatened to report him to the chancellor. 'Sir Thomas despises my father,' the boy replied. 'How could a fine Berber charger be friends with a bristly boar?' Shocked, I put my hand over his mouth; but he tossed his long soft curls out of his face and ran off with a hard laugh.

I could not help being astonished at the delicate insight which childish inexperience often has into the secrets of the emotions. For truly Sir Thomas never gave any hint of an antipathy toward the king or was in any way remiss in respectful decorum.

Every evening this indispensable man sat at the royal table and cheered the king with the subtle play of his speech. I can still see Sir Henry listening intently to every word that fell from the scarcely moving lips. I stood behind my lord's chair, and I studied in silent fear that disembodied face that was equally pale by lamplight and sunshine. For me, even in the lively moods of the banquet, it never wholly vanished—the mark of death that had stared at me from that face when it lay beside Grace's head on the casket cushion.

Have you seen that picture from Byzantium that the monks in All Hallows' monastery in Schaffhausen guard as their greatest treasure? It shows the dead Savior, with sunken eyes and closed eyelids; but if it is looked at closely for a time its expression changes, and through some artistry of drawing and the distribution of the shadows it looks at you with opened, sorrowing eyes. A dishonest art, sir canon! A painter should draw his lines clearly and not ambiguously.

With the chancellor it was the other way. If I looked at his face for a long time, especially if he was silent, it seemed that his eyelids had been closed and a dead man was sitting at the king's table.

I am not certain of it, sir, but I believe that during those days the king may have opened his heart to the chancellor about the grief for which he was involuntarily responsible. Even if it was only with a few veiled words, I think he had declared his regret and his sorrow. He tried to shake off the burden from himself and, I believe, onto my shoulders. I did not hold it against him, because that is the way of the world, and I was not endangered by it. The chancellor was much too wise to confuse a weapon and the hand that wielded it, and much too exalted to consider a servant worthy of his vengeance.

Understand me: King Henry may have blamed and cursed an accident of fate, and me, for the sad death of the child. The pillaging of the girl, the lusts of his flesh he did not place very high in any account of his own misdeeds, for he acknowledged no justice and no law in such affairs. Further, I believe, he was taking the whole matter rather lightly, since the Judge of us all had not yet placed it in the balance in its full weight.

DURING THAT time it happened that after a hunt the chancellor came riding up behind the king, and the two rested under a large, shady oak. I sat on the sunlit side of the trunk and scratched one of the hunting dogs behind the ears. The king knew that I was trustworthy, and he was accustomed to be unrestrained in my presence. Sir Thomas usually looked right past me; when his glance fell on me it was not unfriendly, because that verse from the Koran I spoke beside Grace's coffin had pleased and comforted him. Thus I witnessed a remarkable conversation that seems incredible in terms of human understanding; but it is as literally true and certain as that I am sitting here beside you.

The two men were discussing a document from the king of France which the chancellor had pulled forth from his robes. He was carrying on at that time a secret correspondence with the Capetian in Paris, on the subject of finding a replacement for his chancellor, Abbot Suger, who had recently died. The French king would have been delighted to have Sir Thomas desert King Henry and then lure him as the shrewdest man on earth into his own service. Sir Thomas had acted as though he might not be unwilling, and he exploited this unsought-for situation to learn in the most direct and authoritative way what he needed to know about the French king's attempts against Thomas's own king and the Norman crown in general.

In the letter that the chancellor handed to King Henry, the French king again pressed him to transfer his services. My lord enjoyed the letter with a truly regal delight.

'Just look,' he said mockingly, 'he is offering ten thousand pounds. He is willing to pay high. But nothing will come of it, my dear French cousin; I will never give up this man, a good bargain at any price!' He laid his hand lovingly upon his favorite's shoulder. Then he went on, joking, in a reckless, cocksure mood: 'If you have anything against me in your heart, Thomas, to require me to make compensation for—very well; here is the way for you to do it, valiantly but also with no risk to life and limb. Tomorrow I am sending you, on the matter that you know about, to Paris, to the one who is trying to enlist you. Let us see if he succeeds in tempting you and luring you into your debasement with his flattery.'

Do not be too surprised at this injudicious jesting and the king's shameless self-confidence. You could understand it if you saw the two of them sitting there side by side—the powerful body and leonine head of one, the delicate limbs and gentle demeanor of the other.

A silence ensued. I believe that the chancellor felt it bitterly when Sir Henry, who was so much in his debt, thoughtlessly and cruelly mocked his innate tractability and submissiveness, which after all was wholly for the king's advantage and benefit. After a slight pause Sir Thomas replied without any sign of vexation, in a quiet and—how shall I say it?—philosophical vein: 'Whatever I might have against you, my master, little or much, you have good reason not to doubt my loyalty. I am neither so wicked nor so shortsighted and unstable that I would become a traitor. But your jesting wisdom has touched my sore point. For you know my imperfect character and my nature which inclines toward humility and being of service. Whether it comes from being accustomed early in life to serving a lord, or is a trait of my people's heritage, I cannot resist the annointed head of kings.

'And since you are in a happy mood and showing benevolence toward your servant, he ventures to speak a word of advice in this confidential solitude: Never give me away into the hand of a master who is more powerful than you. For in my ignominious submissiveness I would have to be obedient to him in every respect, even against you, O King of England. But I am talking nonsense! For where is the king who could be mightier than you? What sovereign could quarrel against you without suffering damage and loss? For no living being could summon you to judgment. So I am speaking nonsense and talking about something that does not exist, something that is only a dream, a breath, a nothing.'

The king probably held no higher opinion of this speech than the chancellor's characterization of it, for after he had pondered a little, he yawned as if the whole thing were a pointless and unpleasant comment. He ordered me to get him a goblet of wine.

I too could make nothing of the chancellor's remarks. Only later I came to the conclusion that the mortally wounded man was referring, covertly and hesitantly, to the mysterious and slow vengeance of God.

King Henry raised the goblet, contemplated the golden gleam of the Rhine wine, as if its clarity delighted his soul. He drained the strong drink in one gulp and then laughed until the tears flowed.

'How you impress me, my Thomas!' the king stammered indistinctly, for he had drunk the wine on an empty stomach and it was going to his head. 'More and more illustrious all the time! On my faith—I don't know what I'm saying—it would give me no small pleasure to hang a little mass bell around your scrawny neck and in the Devil's name set you in one bound on the throne at Canterbury! Sit on that throne, and issue your pronouncements against the Holy Father!'

The chancellor stood up more quickly than was his habit. 'It isn't good to sit under this oak. It may be that in ancient times terrible magic was performed here. Its shade confuses the brain.'

Here the conversation ended.

EVEN IN THE humor of drunkenness my lord and king had not totally missed the mark in thinking that the chancellor sometimes indulged in strange, melancholy contemplations. I myself knew something about that.

There was an anteroom where I often waited for the

king for hours, and where occasionally the chancellor would pace back and forth, deep in thought, paying no attention to me. In a dark corner hung a large wooden crucifix. It was a rude, thin piece of sculpture, but it had a head with touching pathetic features. The king held this crucifix in the greatest esteem, because his ancestor, William the Conqueror, had prayed to it before the battle of Hastings and had been victorious with its help.

Formerly the chancellor had avoided letting his fastidious eyes rest on the statue, I suppose because he abominated trickling blood and ugliness. But in these days I was amazed to hear him sometimes talking to the brown crucifix. He whispered to it, but I could clearly hear that it was in Arabic. I rejoiced that he was turning to the Good Comforter, although there was something uncanny about it that made me uneasy. Sir, I heard too little and too much: I heard things I would rather not repeat—things that would not endanger your soul but would be a vexation to your piety. After all, I couldn't be sure how far the chancellor had put away Moorish customs and whether he, like us, was calling on the Blessed One on the cross as the Lord God himself. All I heard were a few deep sighs, some disconnected words in the language that was gradually fading from my memory—some words that edified or horrified me. He spoke fervently and sorrowfully to the unanswering Crucified One, but—it seemed to me— blasphemously and as if to a fellow being.

One day the chancellor was standing in front of the statue, unaware of my presence, for I was sitting silent on a footstool in a corner of the large room, doing nothing to attract attention. 'You, too, have suffered,' he breathed, 'and probably just as horribly as you are shown hanging here, in torment. Why? Why? The Writings say it was to bear the sins of the world. What had you done to atone for, you heavenly spirit? You were to bring peace and good will to men. But behold! The earth still reeks and stinks with blood and horror. And both guilt and innocence are being murdered as before your time!

'They beat you, spat on you, tortured you. But you persevered in the courage of love, and on the cross you prayed for your killers. Banish the vulture of unreconciled grief that devours my heart, so that I may walk in your footsteps! I am the poorest and most pitiful of mortals. Lo,

I belong to you and cannot part from you, you patient king of scorned and crucified mankind!'

After the chancellor had been whispering to the statue, he turned slowly and discovered me on my footstool. I behaved as if nothing had happened and resolved to lie staunchly if he should ask me if I had heard him.

But he approached me with quiet steps, with an almost imperceptible smile. 'Son of Japheth,' he addressed me, 'you have lived among the children of Shem, and you know that they do not believe the Eternal let his only son be nailed to the cross. How do you teach them, to set them aright?'

I lifted my eyes to the chancellor, looked steadfastly at him and answered firmly: 'My Savior kissed Judas the betrayer and forgave his tormenters. A mere human being cannot do that; it is against nature and human character.'

Sir Thomas nodded quietly. 'You have spoken truly,' he declared; 'it is difficult, it is impossible.'

THE WORDS of the chancellor may not have been wholly orthodox, but his works became more and more Christian. It seemed as if in those days Sir Thomas was weary of magnificence and wanted to divest himself of splendor and, himself a heartsick man without peace, wanted to heal wounds and bring peace as far as was within his power. But he did this cautiously, so that the king and the Normans would not ridicule him or distrust him.

It was not hard for him to show the king that it would be wise not to burden the Saxons excessively and thus drive them to despair, and that it would be advantageous for him to stand there above them as a kindly being— more generous than his Normans, who mistreated their Saxon servants and maids as they pleased. Thus he was able to relieve the Saxons through royal laws, not conspicuously and provocatively, but discreetly and quietly so as not to irritate the Normans. You understand, sir, he repacked the burden on the mule's back without reducing it, and he merely saw to it that the straps did not cut too deeply into the flesh.

But he also did favors for the Normans and redoubled his generosity toward them. He overwhelmed them with goodwill and princely gifts and settled their personal quarrels with wise words of decision. If two important

67

people had fallen out, he intervened as a peacemaker between them. 'Who am I,' he would say, 'to meddle in the affairs of the great? The king's servant, who wants to maintain for him the pillars of his throne.' And the two adversaries left, reconciled and their pride satisfied.

If only Sir Fauconbridge had taken warning! He envied the chancellor the goodwill he enjoyed with both kings, Sir Henry and the Capetian, and lay in wait for him with sword and slander. He forged the chancellor's handwriting in letters to the king of France, on the basis of which he charged Sir Thomas with treason, while he himself was spinning risky plots at the French court.

Sir Thomas saw through all this and kept watch on him. He invited him—I carried the letter myself—without informing and disquieting the king, and presented him with the truth serenely and with incontrovertible proofs. Since he let Sir Fauconbridge go his way, without destroying him with one blow as he could have, the Norman considered him a cautious coward and behaved after that with redoubled impudence and sense of security, until he infringed on the crown with an act which was an unmistakable felony. Then of course his scaffold had to be erected.

In that way Sir Fauconbridge, whose ancestors had come over with the Conqueror, forfeited his heritage and his head, because of the chancellor's long-suffering compassion.

When he later told the king that he had recognized the rebellious baron's moves from the beginning, the king asked why he had not unmasked the traitor sooner. The chancellor's reply was: 'O King, to what purpose? Invisible arms stir under everyone's actions. Everything comes to fruition in due time, and each of us is at last overtaken by his appointed hour.'

Chapter Eight

"ONE DAY THE king and his chancellor were sitting in a castle in Normandy, discussing political matters. The king had a goblet filled with the light champagne that he loved; and the chancellor was outlining to him the contents of the courier's pouch which had just arrived from England. He kept until last one letter, from which the seal of Canterbury dangled. Speaking in his quiet way he unfolded it as the king looked on. He reported: 'The primate of Canterbury died early last week, sire.' King Henry was not particularly surprised. Without commenting, he continued to look at the chancellor, benevolently. 'He has been ailing for quite a while,' Sir Thomas went on, 'but I did not think he was so close to the end. Now the hour of decision has come for you, O King, and for the government of England. It is the proper time for you to remove your kingdom's malignant ulcer, the ecclesiastical jurisdiction, and bring healing to the realm. If my king fills this dangerous office by a bold choice, he has come close to the fulfillment of his royal wishes.'

The king's eyes twinkled mischievously. Perhaps it was because he took pleasure in his chancellor's wisdom, as usual; perhaps he hoped that this time he could outdo him and take him by surprise.

Sir Thomas saw the king's sly expression and observed it coolly. 'We could not ask for a more favorable pope than the one they elevated to the throne in Rome a few months ago. He has a passion through which we can approach the human side of him. With the eagerness of a connoisseur, he collects and studies coins. Strange to say, while he is content with a few well-preserved specimens from the Roman Empire, he is insatiable about your gold coins, sir. He yearns to have hundreds, indeed thousands of them, because they bear the likeness of your exalted countenance, in which he takes delight as that of a loyal son of the church.'

King Henry shook with laughter, while the chancellor delivered this scornful speech with the serious sad expression he always had when he was joking. 'But how will my lord fill the throne of the primate?' he went on. 'With this abbot or that bishop?'—I am no longer certain of the names, and I would not mislead you for anything in the world—'They are both well-suited for Your Majesty's purposes, but perhaps the abbot would be better, since he is the more vicious.'

'Then he would be easier to control,' the king agreed with the chancellor's meaning.

'The bishop would be just as pliant,' Sir Thomas replied. 'The advantage of the abbot is something different, and I am merely supplying words for my king's wisdom, if I expose the dangers of your policy as follows. You know, sire, how and why your exalted and glorious ancestor, the Conqueror, granted the English bishoprics jurisdiction not only over the legal transactions involving the clergy but also over lawsuits between clerics and laymen, thus weakening and disrupting the state. At the time that was useful, since the first bishops were the creatures of the Conqueror. But now it is harmful; it is intolerable. For all the willfulness of your Normans stoops down behind the protection of a bishop's crosier, and every rebel against Your Majesty has his head shaved and then laughs with impunity at the lightnings of your justice.'

My lord the king was a friend of justice and order; his hand on the arm of his chair became a clenched fist.

'It is not concealed from your wisdom,' Sir Thomas observed, 'why even those privileges of the church which were obtained surreptitiously are so difficult to abate or abolish: it is because the church is a twofold thing that consists of a body and a soul. The body is an army of tonsured unmarried men, several thousand cathedrals and monasteries, a bundle of customs, vows, and claims resting on fables and forgeries. The soul of the church is virtue, humility, compassion, chastity'—the king involuntarily made a gesture and his forehead twitched—'in short, all the teachings of that Other One whom they crucified.'

I must tell you, Sir Burkhard, that the chancellor never referred to the Savior by one of the revered names, but always only as the Other One. I suppose it was the reluctance of his heathen blood to pronounce the holy name.

'The people, sire, cannot distinguish between the vessel and its contents. If you deal with a primate who can exert authority over the English soul through his virtue, you will never deprive him of one iota of his privileges. Therefore you should choose a notorious sinner, one indisputably depraved, like our abbot.'"

THUS THE bowman was continuing in full swing with the chancellor's speech; but Sir Burkhard had leaned forward to him and plucked at his sleeve: "Bowman," he protested, "I consider you a truthful man. But I find it hard to believe that during his lifetime and even before his conversion one who is now a member of the church triumphant could have spoken so disdainfully about the church militant here below, and given your king such impious advice. I have told you that I am not well disposed toward the new saint; but too much is too much. That part is an invention of your own!"

"Sir," replied Hans the Englishman with a wicked smile behind his gray beard, "it can be that the chancellor did not pronounce those exact words at that exact time. But as for the intent, he expressed himself in those terms, you can believe me, and not once but a hundred times—speaking of the political side of things, you understand. He often discussed this question with my king. But it is not impossible that something of my own may have crept in, for unfortunately we can all recite the same litany when the morals of the clergy are talked about—of course with due exception of your institution and especially your own venerated person.

But even assuming that my story may have turned slightly inaccurate, from now on it will be genuine and incontestable as the gospel. For what was said thereafter is fixed in my gray old head like the Roman inscriptions on upturned milestones, whose fragments still bear the

71

indelibly engraved letters. I swear to you by the mercy of the Mother of God, I am speaking the truth. But where was I, when you interrupted me?"

"That vicious abbot of yours," the old man answered, still somewhat irritated.

"Have no doubt that the chancellor recommended him," Hans continued vigorously. "'O King,' said Sir Thomas, 'this animal will in no way be able to defend the privileges of his throne as God-given. You will be able to take them from him—and then away with him!'

He almost spat out the words, contemptuously, from his delicate lips. He added: 'The filthy wretch will destroy himself. He is not content with keeping mistresses like your other bishops; he waylays and ruins innocent youth.'

I think the chancellor had in mind only that notorious lecher. But I thought of Grace, and the king too stirred uneasily. But he quickly overcame any sense of remorse and dismissed any suspicion. After all, he knew that Sir Thomas would have disdained unveiling his inner thoughts by innuendo.

In the cheerful mood of a generous man who is on the point of bestowing a great gift, the king continued with a look of radiant joy: 'What are you thinking of, Thomas? The throne, in which two saints and scholars have sat, one of whom, the blessed Lanfranc, overcame the heretic Berengar who denied transubstantiation; the other, Saint Anselm, who reasoned out a triumphant proof of the existence of God—appoint a swine to that throne? Far be it from my royal will!' And my lord and king was delighted at the knowledge he had of what he intended to do.

A reproachful look came over the chancellor's face, as if he were asking whether Sir Henry would thwart long-pondered plans through a sudden whim.

The king grasped his goblet and emptied it happily. 'I plan to install a primate over my priests that will astonish them: a man of noble and spotless morals, a supersubtle philosopher, and on top of that a man devoted to me and a born foe of the papacy.'

Sir Thomas replied with an incredulous smile: 'My gaze sweeps over your clergy, sire, but it seeks in vain for the one you have chosen.'

'Can't you guess?' the king urged. 'I will help you. I say

to you: truly no one shall sit on the primate's throne but you!'

The chancellor said nothing, but gradually every tint of color retreated from his face. He leaned back in the chair. Then, being careful to avoid looking at the king, he turned his dark eyes to me, at his side. With two fingers of his right hand, which had been hanging relaxed, he lifted a fold of his purple gown and revealed the curled-back tips of his costly shoes.

'Bowman,' he said jovially, and he cast a contemptuous glance over his clothes, agleam with precious stones, 'behold a holy man! This John the Baptist who despises the soft garments they wear at royal courts—behold him, and examine carefully this good shepherd who carries home the strayed lamb on his shoulders, and lays down his life for his herd.'

The king gave a high-pitched laugh, but I had a sick feeling.

Meanwhile the chancellor had turned toward the king, his face cold. 'Your Highness,' he said, 'you cannot be in earnest about that choice. It is impossible in the eyes of your bishops, of your Normans, of your Saxons. Is an English cleric to obey as his father a pliant courtier because in his youth he received the first consecration in holy orders, either by accident or for the sake of some advantage? Shall a Saxon tend the souls of your Normans? Shall a renegade, as they call him, tend the souls of your Saxons? Sir, your chancellor advises you against that bad choice.'

'It is the best one,' King Henry insisted stubbornly. 'With you on the throne of Canterbury, the throne of Saint Peter cracks in all its joints; with you under a mitre, the one on the Holy Father's head will wobble! Check and checkmate!'

The chancellor continued with a serious kind of jocularity. 'I do not know whether you have heard of the changes that can take place in a human being who changes his costume and puts on ecclesiastical raiment. It is no light matter to grasp the shepherd's crook that two now in glory once held in their hands: the blessed Lanfranc, who recognized the fruit of the grain and of the vine as God's body and blood, and the blessed Anselm, who fathomed the unfathomable. Suppose that I became a true

73

bishop, by some miracle. That could be unexpected and unwelcome to you.'

'Thomas, bridle your tongue!' The king shook a threatening finger at him. 'I will not put up with derision of holy things. I have long since seen through you: you have absorbed Arabic philosophy; you are a follower of some esoteric doctrine; you are not a humble Christian. But I am; I wish to live and die a Christian!'

'You cannot believe, O King,' said Sir Thomas pointing to his breast, 'that upon this withered tree the dew of Heaven may yet fall—and you are right! But it is possible to grow weary of the world even without piety. Under the wings of your might I have governed this realm many years—with what devices? With violence, bribes, breaches of faith—and worse, that I prefer not to mention. Thus the kingdoms of this world are managed. But I am tired of it. What is this England to me? I am not a Norman; I am not even a Saxon! Foreign blood flows in my veins. And the treasures with which you, O generous king, have loaded me—for whom do I gather them? For rust and moths.'

I saw at once that Sir Thomas was thinking of Grace's death, and the king too was moved. A tear rolled down his cheek, for Sir Henry had a soft heart.

'*Sunt lacrimae rerum*,' the chancellor murmured to himself. 'Whose verse is that, Armorer? You were a cleric.' He turned to me again, as if he wished to resume the mask of equanimity that had been dropped for an instant.

'It is a line from the Roman poet Vergil,' I answered at once, 'and it means that the affairs of mortals must not be put under too great a strain, for within they are full of tears.' Thus I tried to come to the aid of my lord and king.

'Take from me the old yoke,' the chancellor begged, 'instead of imposing a new one upon me, one which would put me in an unseemly, ambiguous situation.'

Look for another chancellor? Impossible; Sir Thomas was indispensable. He could not mean it seriously. I had to conclude that King Henry must have been saying this to himself, for he suddenly broke out with the words: 'You are ambitious, ambitious, ambitious! You set a high price on yourself, you arrogant man, because you know

74

you are irreplaceable. Thomas, I don't like that. A cheerful giver deserves a cheerful receiver.'

'I must remain your chancellor, because I believe our stars and the hours of our births stand in connection with each other,' Sir Thomas answered, 'but do not force me to be your archbishop!'

'Take hold, take hold!' the king shouted, on fire at this first sign of yielding. 'Hold back, O King,' the chancellor called out at the same time, and with a look, reverend sir, that I will never forget—the look of a dying man. He brushed his hand across his forehead as if a wound were burning there, and his voice sank to a whisper: 'Where am I being led? Into what doubts? Into what service and obedience? Into what death?'

Then he raised his voice again to ask, almost threateningly: 'Are you sure of me, O King?'

'Surer than I am of myself,' King Henry affirmed. The king's hearing was not keen and he had not heard the whispered words. 'Enough of mysteries! I need you, Thomas. And don't ask what England means to you. My favor has long since raised you above the Saxons, and I have done more for you than for any Norman.'

Here a flash of derision came and went across the chancellor's face. But King Henry paid no attention to it and shouted impatiently: 'No more objections! I will exalt you as high as I want to, and you will obey!'

Then Sir Thomas bowed his head and spoke. 'What you decree—let it come to pass.'

Chapter Nine

"THEN IN obedience to his master the chancellor traveled back to England, with absolute power of royal authority. With his skillful fingers he shaped and molded like yielding clay the bishops who were to elect the primate, until they emerged from his masterly hand as his creatures and their votes were unanimous in his favor. Everything went well. Sir Thomas was named, and the Norman bishop of Winchester bestowed his fraternal blessing on him with great solemnity and a bittersweet expression.

Then one day an incredible story reached Normandy. It was reported to my lord and king that his chancellor had divested himself of all the pomp of worldly life, at one stroke and totally. For the traditional banquet at his episcopal consecration, against all propriety and custom, he had invited not only his brothers, the bishops, and other aristocratic clergymen along with the flower of Norman nobility, but he had also had the poor and the sick, beggars and cripples, brought in from the highways and hedgerows to fill his great halls and the bishop's board fittingly.

The king considered this story an invention or at least an exaggeration by envious enemies of his favorite. He made merry at the expense of his Norman courtiers, who were displeased at this unprecedented and scandalous thing. 'Gentlemen,' he teased them, 'you have to give credit to my chancellor; he knows the proprieties of demeanor and costume appropriate to every situation. He shows flawless taste in everything! He outshone you in the courtier's perfections and excelled all of you in fine knightly manners. Now he is giving his new colleagues, the bishops, the lofty example of genuine apostolic conduct. A rare man—truly a unique man!'

New reports confirmed the first, with the additional information that the primate had laid aside his costly bishop's garb immediately after his installation and was wandering with an emaciated face through the streets in a coarse cowl, followed wherever he walked or stood by his guests, the Saxon beggars. King Henry grew uncertain, and his joking impulses subsided. Soon, however, he had guessed that the incomparably clever man was merely assuming a mask of holiness in order to have a strong bargaining position against the pope in the forthcoming negotiations about the clerical jurisdiction in England. Even so, he resolved to look into the whole matter with his own eyes for himself, and he hastened his return to England.

ON THE WAY from Dover to London he was repeatedly addressed by Norman noblemen calling for their rights against the new primate, his chancellor, who was refusing to return to them their runaway Saxon servants, who—as the nobles complained—were now rushing in large numbers to the cloisters to get their heads shaved, whereupon King Henry shook his, disgruntled.

On the morning after he arrived in Windsor all the nobility gathered in the great hall of the castle to greet His Majesty's return. He was still asleep. I kept watch at the door through which the king was accustomed to enter the hall and from where the glittering gathering could be easily observed.

Among all the gentlemen there was talk of nothing else than the inexplicable sudden transformation of Sir Thomas. They awaited his appearance impatiently; they knew that he would come to greet the king, and they were talking animatedly but with lowered voices, as is fitting in the halls of royalty. Only Sir Rollo, who towered over all of them by a head, did not restrain himself; his speech rumbled like a hollow roll of thunder.

He stood on the right side of the hall in a circle of old gentlemen, the leanest and most dried-up figure among them, and in his characteristic way he abused the whole tonsured crowd and the new primate in particular.

'I never gave him credit for manly honesty,' the old armorer inveighed, 'that pale coward. The disloyal and fainthearted slave is sneaking his skinny body into a monk's cowl because he thinks he is safer there than under the protection of his king. If only I had picked a fight with the hypocrite while he was wearing a sword! You wait and see: that schemer will stir up plenty of trouble for us.' And the gentlemen agreed with him.

On the other side of the hall the younger aristocrats were sneering and snickering at Sir William Tracy's caricature sketchbook. That gentleman, you must know, was an accomplished artist who could ridicule with his pencil better than anyone else. By means of a slight distortion he could change a human countenance into the face of an animal or the likeness of something inanimate, exposing it to the laughter of all who saw it. That pencil once got hold of me and pictured me as a bowlegged retriever bringing the king a woodcock in my huge jaws. Although I didn't enjoy the joke, I was the first to laugh, because that was the wise thing to do. Others, more irritable and of higher rank than I, probably were angered when Sir William sketched their distorted likeness on the tablets of his book, which he wore on a chain at his belt. It was well for him that his sword was as sharp as his stylus; otherwise the sharpness of the latter could have cost him his life.

The scoffer was showing the younger knights a new drawing. I was curious about it: I approached Sir Reginald the handsome, as he was called, who had the book in his hand at the moment. He bent double with laughter and dropped the book on the floor. I picked it up for him and caught sight of a strange plant. There was a thin stalk with drooping leaves that formed the sleeves of a monk's robe. The unsteady stalk became a neck on which grew, instead of an ear of grain, a familiar face—a martyr's face. It was the face of a hypocritical hermit, and the very image of the primate.

In so short a time, at a court, a man everyone feared becomes a laughingstock.

The little book was still making its rounds when an unusual sound was heard in the distance. It was a simple

79

devout litany, which slowly approached the castle courtyard, sung by thousands of fervent voices. It was partly a
battle cry, partly a lamentation.

'The primate and his beggars!' was the cry in the hall,
and the gentlemen hurried to the windows. I found an
opening and saw Sir Rollo on the nearest battlement
stretch out his mailed right hand imperiously.

'Raise the drawbridge! Close the gate!' he shouted down
into the courtyard, where Norman men-at-arms were
guarding the entrance. But the peaceful throng of monks,
beggars, children, all sorts of people of lower rank, pushed
and forced their way in—irresistibly, like a herd of hungry
cattle. It was too late for the soldiers to obey Sir Rollo;
instinctively they had retreated, for Sir Thomas had
blessed them with outstretched arms. He walked behind a
cross carried aloft at the head of his pitiful procession. He,
whom I had never seen come to the court except in costly
clothes and with the most elegant retinue, now wore a
rough haircloth garment, and the toes of his sandaled feet
shone out from under the dark wool like pieces of ivory.

Respectfully and diffidently the servants of the royal
household received him to escort him into the castle. On
the threshold he turned to his followers and instructed
them to be patient and wait for his return.

They obeyed, and humbly they settled down on the
ground, leaving free the stone benches in the courtyard
and the steps of the marble stairway. My glance fell on the
Saxon who had carried the primate's cross. He was standing in the midst of the crowd, holding high the symbol
entrusted to him. Most of his clay-colored face was covered by a red beard, but still I thought I could recognize
those coarse features. Truly, it was Trustan Grimm, the
fiancé of Hilde, the bowmaker's daughter in London. I
was happy that he had become a monk, and I surmised
that Hilde had rejected him, despite her humiliation and
the wishes of her father. Later on I learned that this was
indeed the case.

Meanwhile Sir Thomas had climbed the inner stairway,
and he was just entering the hall as I turned away from
the window. He was the target of all eyes as he walked
quietly to the middle of the room. He slowly looked
around at the gathering and with a fatherly gesture raised
his right hand in blessing. A murmur of displeasure ran

through the group. The denunciation of the armorer could be heard above the general murmur: 'Keep it for yourself, priest, your shabby blessing; we don't want it.'

Sir Thomas silently turned toward the open window, where, scorned by the Normans, he extended his right hand compassionately over the Saxon people below. Then there rose from the depths of the courtyard a clamor, a cry of weeping and joy, so that the rejoicing could not be distinguished from the lamentation. For since the Saxons had lost their native kings, it was the first time in a century that a greeting and blessing had been bestowed on them from a royal window.

But the Normans clenched their fists and some grasped the pommel of their swords.

Paying no attention to anyone, the primate turned to the familiar door just as a chamberlain was opening it from within. King Henry stepped into the hall in a fine morning mood. Sir Thomas stood before him respectfully and waited to be spoken to, his head lowered in an attitude of submission.

King Henry studied the chancellor for a time, attentively and dubiously, much as—bear with me when I say it—much as one inspects a long-time favorite horse or hunting dog whose appearance has been oddly changed by being clipped or having its tail docked. Surprise and laughter were visible on his face, but he remembered his royal dignity and first he dismissed the courtiers with an affable gesture.

'We thank you, gentlemen,' he said, 'for your greeting, your readiness to serve, your love. We can save the joy and jollities of reunion for our festive table, to which we invite all of you as beseems our goodwill and your merits. But first comes business with our chancellor. Be pleased to stroll through our new gardens. And don't fail to notice the fountain in the rear courtyard, the fierce lion head that the Walloon master has completed for us in our absence. Au revoir, seigneurs barons!'

After these words by the king the hall was emptied. The last to leave was the armorer, Sir Rollo, who strode out reluctantly.

Now my lord and king could no longer restrain himself. 'Good God, Thomas, how you do look!' he teased his chancellor. 'Have you been molting? Your feathers have fallen off, you have kicked off the rams' horns of your knightly shoes. I see you have even lost your shoes too! Well, well! Anything can happen with a philosopher like you! Surely you haven't shed your glittering skin like a snake? Granted that a certain amount of abstinence is becoming in a bishop, you—you man of extremes—you are doing too much of a good thing, much too much. Are you trying to mortify the flesh like a desert ascetic? The way you look, I won't be able to dine with you, which was always a delight for me. But water and roots aren't good for a royal stomach.'

Sir Thomas listened to these jolly words with lowered head and unchanged expression. Then he raised his eyes to the king's face. My lord could see how the strict fasting and cruel punishing of the flesh had wasted the bishop's cheeks, sharpened the outline of his skull and given his gaze, which was always serious, a strangely inward look.

Compassion overwhelmed my lord. 'Thomas, my dear Thomas,' he began again, 'throw this mask away. We are alone and unobserved. I realize that this mummery is for my own best interests; but I'll be damned if I see what your purpose is. Open your mouth, you riddle, you mystery.'

'Your speech, my lord and king, takes me by surprise,' answered the chancellor. 'I am no other than what I seem to be and behave as being—your servant, whom you know.'

'Am I bewitched?' the king exclaimed. 'Is this my hand? Am I the king? Are you my chancellor? Have we sat together, day after day, and ruled this land? No, let us carry this untimely joking no further. This isn't a carnival eve: it is clear, sober sunlight. What weird spirit has gotten into you? Pour out your heart to me. You know that mine is always open to you!'

'I thank you, O King, that you encourage your creature to speak freely with you,' the primate answered. 'Here I dare confess to you that this hand is not strong enough to carry at the same time the bishop's crook and your privy seal. Inevitably one or the other of the treasures entrusted to me would suffer damage. I am too loyal a servant to wish an unserviceable chancellor for you or a bad bishop for the church. I implore you, sir—this token which your mighty will vouchsafed to entrust to me as

82

your instrument, this pledge of your boundless undeserved favor which was mine for years—take it back from
me today!'

And Sir Thomas reached into the folds of his robe, now
too large for him. He took out the royal seal with the
three leopards and held it out to the king, to put it into his
hand.

'By no means!' cried King Henry, stepping back. 'We
made no such bargain, chancellor! I cannot do without
you a single hour. Only you and your cleverness can ac-
complish what we have dreamed of and watched over
together. With my powerful hand I could wreck the delicate web of your fingers. No resistance! You are and you
remain my chancellor.'

'You do not wish my ruin,' Sir Thomas entreated him;
'you are too magnanimous for that. But see! I have not the
courage to bear the wrath of that Higher One into whose
hands you have given me. He is a jealous master, who
suffers no second beside Himself!'

This speech was hard to interpret: it so confused the
king that he took back the seal without knowing what he
was doing. He wrinkled his forehead suspiciously and his
voice had a discordant sound: 'To whom, then, have I
relinquished you? Surely not the pope in Rome?'

The primate shook his head in denial. A light, not of
this world, suddenly shone from his brow. He lifted his
thin arm, and the sleeve of his robe fell back; and he
pointed upward. The king was astounded and frightened
to the depths of his soul. The seal slipped from his hand
and fell to the floor with a clanging crash. I stepped forward and bent over to the precious instrument, whose
knob was of pure gold. When I picked it up, I saw that it
was cracked. A tiny split ran right through the gem bearing the coat of arms of England. Silently I placed it on the
table with the four dragon's-foot legs which stood next to
the king's chair.

When I turned again to the two, my lord had composed
himself. He said with forced joviality: 'Saint George preserve me! You gave me a real fright, Thomas. But now
enough of these surprises and little tricks! Sit down here
with me, and let us get to work on these tiresome business matters, the way we always do.'

He threw himself into his chair, and I brought up

another one, a little lower but just as richly ornamented, for the chancellor—the chair in which he always sat beside the king.

But Sir Thomas remained standing at a respectful distance before the king. 'Illustrious sir, give me time and be patient!' he said. 'I used half a lifetime to search into the relationships and laws of your kingdom. How could I learn overnight those of the holy church, in whose service you have put me, and to which I have long been an outsider, indeed a hostile outsider? Therefore bear with me!'

'Down to business, Thomas, down to business! You know perfectly well why I made you my primate. Let us work together to annul and destroy ecclesiastical jurisdiction.'

'You will find me favorably disposed,' the archbishop answered, thoughtfully. 'But these privileges that are in dispute are, in my eyes, fluctuating forms, changing configurations, earthen vessels, serviceable or useless, depending on whether they preserve in purity the wine of eternal justice or poison it. I plan to turn to the master himself with questions of his intention.'

'To whom will you go for guidance, Thomas?' the king laughed, 'the Holy Trinity?'

'In the Gospels,' Sir Thomas whispered; 'from Him who was found free of any injustice.'

'No bishop talks like that!' cried Sir Henry in honest indignation, 'only an evil heretic uses such language! The revered Gospels belong on an altar cloth embroidered with pearls; they have no bearing on worldly matters and realities. Look me in the eye, Thomas! Either you are trying to become my enemy, or your senseless fasting has beclouded the glorious clarity of your mind. To be brief: destroy the ecclesiastical jurisdiction, Thomas! For that purpose, for that purpose alone, I put you on my splendid throne of Canterbury. I do not want to leave unavenged the sinfulness of my clergy and thereby call down the lightnings of God's judgment upon myself and my house. Just recently a Saxon cleric blasphemed treasonably in the pulpit against the works and fame of my ancestor, the Conqueror, and a Norman priest violated a child's innocence.'

'Sir,' replied the primate, and his sunken cheeks flushed, 'be assured that I condemn the sins of my clergy

more severely than any secular court would. Abomina-
tions! And the most abominable'—here he paused and
then concluded with quieter, changed tone—'insurrection
and rebellion against your ancestors and yourself, Christian kings. In such matters I discern God's will clearly.
But whether he commands me to surrender Saxons who
take refuge in my monasteries to their tormentors, your
barons—that I question, that I doubt.'

Now King Henry recognized unmistakably that the
primate would be unwilling to relinquish the ecclesiastical jurisdiction and was mocking him with holiness.

'I have been tricked!' he screamed and jumped up out of
his chair.

At this moment the Saxons waiting in the courtyard
below began a new litany, perhaps in order to calm their
anxiety about the primate. They sang the triumphant
Vexilla Dei prodeunt ["The Banners of God Go Forward"].

King Henry, already irritated, dashed to the window
and looked down. 'Thomas,' he ordered, 'command those
scoundrels that you drag along at your heels to be silent.
The howling of your starving pack disgusts me.'

Sir Thomas did not move. 'Can a bishop forbid the poor
and afflicted to follow the cross?' he asked meekly.

Then the king got into a blind rage. 'You are stirring up
the Saxons, you rebel, you traitor!' he yelled, and took a
step toward the primate. His blue eyes protruded and he
clutched the air with his sinewy fingers as if he would
like to strangle the man standing quietly before him.

A door opened. Queen Eleanor rushed in and threw herself in tears at the primate's feet.

'I am the worst of sinners,' she sobbed, 'and not worthy
to kiss the dust from your sandals, you holy man!'

Sir Thomas bent toward her and soothed her with gentle words. The spectacle restored King Henry's self-control. For quite a while he looked at his wife as she lay
at the bishop's feet. Then he shrugged his shoulders,
laughed aloud, turned his back, and left the hall.

Chapter Ten

"On that day a poison-tipped arrow wounded King Henry's heart. At first the sting was slight, and sometimes it seemed that it would heal. But deep down it kept festering and gnawing at his flesh more and more painfully until from this one point Sir Henry's whole being was undermined and his life as a king was shattered.

Ruin did not overwhelm him all at once, for his strong happy nature resisted it. In the pressure of business, in the ventures and hazards of life he could clench his teeth and forget his grievance. But at night bad dreams plagued him when he had barely fallen asleep. He would jump out of bed and stride restlessly back and forth reproving the ungrateful favorite who haunted and frightened him as a nocturnal specter. Sometimes he sounded hurt and threatening, sometimes affectionate and cajoling. He held up to the ghost all the examples of ingratitude he could recollect from biblical and secular history, and argued that his ingratitude was the greatest. No mouth can describe what my king suffered. Sir Thomas pursued him, present or absent.

If the primate stood bodily before the king as a patient sufferer, Sir Henry became furious at the pitiable sight. If Sir Thomas stayed away from the king in the tranquillity of his episcopal residence, Sir Henry was angry and complained even more heart-rendingly that the one closest to him, the one who knew him as no one else did, was keeping away from him and turning against him the keen edge of a superhuman intelligence.

And yet the primate was not remiss in offering words of reconciliation and submissive willingness to meet the king halfway. Then the king would rush headlong and hastily grasp the tentatively offered hand, which the primate, frightened at this triumphant grasping, withdrew again, chilled. My king could just as well have embraced a cloud as held on to his former chancellor, that slender, supple eel.

But even when the primate was willing to make a genuine and substantial concession about an issue, somehow things didn't work out. Either on the way to Windsor he would encounter an unworldly hermit, who had to choose just that day to crawl out of his cave and beseech the beloved bishop not to surrender the laws of God and abandon his children, the poor, to the princes of this world. Or a monk in a fit of ecstasy, brandishing a cross, would bar his way only a few paces from the royal threshold and drive the meek primate back to Canterbury with fanatical words.

Would you like to learn the truth? In my opinion a compromise formula may well have existed or could have been contrived by the chancellor's shrewdness—a formula that would have protected and assured equally the royal authority and the rights of a merciful church. After all, the king was not inhumane, and Sir Thomas was not a hot-headed zealot. But the two men's hearts had become strangers to each other, and whenever they wanted to take that last step to meet, their dead former affection came between them as a pale shade of hatred.

Furthermore, be it not forgotten that Queen Eleanor, now a dutiful wife, never budged from my lord's side. Since her conversion she poured into his ears day and night that he must not offend God's saint. In this way she provoked the king yet more and made him all the more obdurate.

Likewise, in accordance with the usages of a court, the king's anger and stubbornness were incited by whisperers who laid fires and blew embers into flame. The entire Norman aristocracy vented its hatred and abhorrence on the godly rebel who was opening the impregnable refuge of his cloisters to the runaway bondsmen of the conquered estates. Daily and hourly the king was kept informed about how the archbishop was mighty and growing mightier among the Saxons, as he stretched out his treacherous hands, bringing help and blessing everywhere and at all times. He was undermining the state, the barons said, by secretly hatching a pious insurrection of souls which was more dangerous than open bodily revolt because it could not be suppressed by weapons. When such insinuations were whispered to the king he would kick his favorite hunting hound in irritation, and he treated me roughly, especially when I handed him one of those subtle letters in which the primate took back with an uneasy left hand what he had given with his magnanimous right hand.

It could happen that the king would curse and crumple the misleading document in his fist and order a hunt, to try to get over his bad humor out in the open country. But he didn't succeed. If a stag was driven toward him and I gave him his crossbow, he saw his tormentor instead of a frightened animal, and groaned, 'Be on guard, Thomas Scrawny-neck!' as he shot, and he pierced the deer's heart.

Finally King Henry made up his mind. He summoned the primate before the tribunal of his barons, had him convicted of high treason and banished forever from all the king's lands. But on the same day that Sir Thomas had to escape overseas like a criminal, Queen Eleanor parted from her husband and left Windsor Castle with a cry of grief that could be heard far and wide.

NOW MY LORD and king kept listening day and night to get news of what Sir Thomas was up to across the sea.

First came the news that at the coast the Capetian had received him with reverence and sought his blessing. Never in his whole life, the French king assured him, had he, a Christian prince, offended a monk, let alone a bishop.

That was King Louis, whom they called the Young, because he had mounted the throne as a beardless boy. The name stuck, since he never managed to achieve a hearty manliness. Lady Eleanor, whom he had brought home as his queen, used to complain bitterly in the wildness of her reckless, high-spirited youth that she had been married off to a monk.

Indeed this king was by nature a friend of the clergy. He entreated the Father of Christendom, with the addition of golden pence, to take up the holy primate's cause against King Henry. Henry was his and his family's hereditary enemy; he hoped to war against him more effectively with the weapons of the church than with his secular ones.

For his part the Holy Father held the balances with an impartial, cautious hand, taking pains to place his favor at any given time in that pan of the scales which was sinking under the weight of the gold put into it. At that time the papal prudence was disadvantageous to my king, since his wars in Ireland were costing him heavily, and less money than formerly was available to him for the Father of Christendom.

Even so the Holy Father hesitated to intercede for Sir Thomas without reservation. He found it impossible to feel a genuine confidence in him. In his mind the former chancellor and the persecuted bishop could not be clearly distinguished. He had repeatedly come to know the chancellor as a crafty diplomat; and it seemed doubtful to him that Sir Thomas was making no use of his skill, but was allowing himself to be pursued like a great apostle of the early church or a visionary heretic of modern times.

I was assured by reliable witnesses, and in the light of my knowledge of Sir Thomas I considered it true, that he had kept his cause pure and a holy one, and kept his hands clean of any stain of treason against his lord and king. I was told that he had made no demands on the pope nor asked from the Capetians anything more than a cell in a cloister where he could lay his head.

Thus, unprotected by the Holy Father and avoiding the Capetian court, he went from cloister to cloister with his pilgrim's staff of misery; often no one knew his whereabouts. While his bodily substance diminished and all but vanished in France, his power and spiritual presence grew in England and stood in the sky like the full moon above the sorrowing Saxons—or, if you prefer, Sir Thomas dwelt in all English huts and hearts like the Christ child in the stable, humble and glorious. There he reigned as king and banished fear from their souls.

With my own eyes I have seen how the Saxons, and even more their wives, after King Henry had passed his sentence upon the primate, denied his majesty respect and obeisance, turning away when he rode by. I still remember one little incident. The king was strolling one day in his gardens that extended along the forest and the river into the open countryside. As usual I was following at some distance. A towheaded Saxon child crawled out of the blossoming shrubbery and got entangled in the king's legs. The king was in a good humor that day. He picked up the boy, petting him and pushing a silver coin into his chubby hand. 'Be sure to keep that, my boy!' he said. Then the mother, who had instinctively hidden in fear and trembling behind a tree, jumped out, and with her eyes ablaze she snatched the coin from the child and threw it with horror into the bushes as if it had been one of the accursed thirty pieces of silver. I hurried to arrest the insolent woman, who was running off with the child in her arms. But King Henry said 'Hans, let her go.' He walked on, sighing and pondering, his mood spoiled.

Day and night my king's plannings and dreams aimed at stripping Sir Thomas of his rank as primate, legally and permanently; he had persuaded himself that the veneration of the Saxons depended on that title. I often saw him racking his brains and brooding about this, with his hand pressed against his forehead. One morning he came out of his room with a triumphant look on his face—he believed he had solved the riddle.

It was on Ascension Day that Sir Henry appeared before an assembly of barons and explained to them that his widely ramified realm needed a second head. By sharing the crown with his first-born he could lighten his cares and his burdens.

The nobles agreed that Prince Henry should share the crown with his father. Their thoughts and intentions may have been good or bad. The Norman bishop of York crowned and anointed the youth. Thereafter followed a banquet worthy of the occasion, and it was then—as I described last year to your brethren, the noble gentlemen of the chapter, and affirmed as true upon my oath—that my lord waited on the young king at the table and handed him the food with his own hands. 'Today I have been freed from a heavy burden!' he exclaimed and shed tears of joy.

Do you understand the craftiness of this arrangement, sir? Do you understand what burden the king thought he had thrown off? You shake your head? Very well, here is the key.

The great privilege, the incomparable jewel in the mitre of Canterbury, was the crowning of the kings of England. The performance of this rite by a different bishop annihilated the dignity of the primate and degraded Sir Thomas. So the king figured, and he seized upon the device of raising the vain Prince Henry to the throne. He believed his first-born would be satisfied to look in the mirror at the glittering crown on his head and have it embroidered on his clothes and his horses' blankets. Wasn't this plan as neat and politically clever as, in the old days, the proposals of his chancellor, who had now withdrawn from the trickiness of the world?

It was a bad idea that King Henry had! He could not have come upon a worse one! That became evident before many weeks had passed. Two disastrous reports reached Windsor on the same day.

The first told that the young king had taken the changeable Prince Geoffrey to Paris with him, under the pretext of taking part in a tournament. In reality it was for the purpose of quite unnecessarily and ignominiously receiving the lands of the Norman realm on the other side of the Channel as a fief from the Capetians.

The other told how on Pentecost Sir Thomas had emerged from hiding and appeared in a French city. Amid the resounding peals of the church bells he had blown out the candles on the high altar of the cathedral with his own breath, interdicting the bishop of York, who had encroached on the rights of the throne of Canterbury. When the old king—for my lord had to bear this unwelcome title after the coronation of his son—received these two messages, he behaved like a man in a frenzy. He raged; he ungirded himself in the presence of his servants; he hurled himself on his bed; he ripped the silken covers to shreds; with his teeth he tore the wool from the pillows; he beat his breast with his fists in desperation.

'Get this vile vampire from my heart!' he roared, foaming at the mouth at the thought of Sir Thomas; 'he is gnawing at me body and soul!'"

SIR BURKHARD had listened to this narrative with displeasure. He was a Ghibelline and loyal to the Holy

Roman Empire, and for that reason he was on the side of a king, even in matters involving other nations. He could take no pleasure in seeing a great and valiant prince so humiliating himself.

He aired his displeasure with a taunt against the case-hardened bowman: "Those two bad tidings, like messages to Job, on the same day? Hans, you are dreaming! There was a full year between them, unless the numbers in the margin of my chronicle are lying."

"Don't bother me with trivial numbers," the armorer said with some resentment. Then, immediately aware of the impoliteness of his words, he added to soften them: "It makes a difference whether a human being is still in the midst of time and everyday work, or death has closed the biography. Once the last grain of sand has rolled down, man steps out of the sequence of days and hours and stands forth as a complete distinct being at the bar of judgment, before God and man. Both are right and wrong —your chronicle and my memory, it with its figures on parchment, I with symbols engraved in my heart.

But do not hold me back! I must finish, dear sir. For I see before me the blood-covered head of a dead man and the scourged back of my king.

Chapter Eleven

"ON THE evening of the day when my lord and king had shamed and debased himself before his servants in his blind rage, I sat saddened and alone on a low wall by the stables, full of shame and grief for my lord. Unexpectedly I felt a rap on my shoulder. Prince Richard had been looking after his horses, and now he swung himself astride the wall beside me in the familiar way he had with servants.

'Hans,' he said without beating around the bush, 'you saw how senselessly and in what an unknightly way my father acted today. I could pray that this day would sink into everlasting darkness! A raging animal! Misery and shame!' Two childish tears ran over his cheeks. 'It's a good thing those rebels, Henry and Geoffrey, didn't see it; they would describe the unhappy man to the French court and any other king as mad and incompetent, unable to control or rule a kingdom any more than his own temper. If things continue this way, or if it gets worse, what an easy game it will be for my dear brothers to snatch the crown from his head and defraud me of my inheritance! But by God's eyes,' he swore, 'it must not continue!'

'Have patience, Prince Richard,' I interrupted, 'and do not desert a sick man. If you want to enter upon your inheritance with assurance, build on God's word that promises long life and possession of the land to those who honor their father and mother.'

'It is not for my sake alone that this thing must end,' said Prince Richard. 'I am the third-born, and on my word of honor I would be happier if I seized a kingdom with my own hand than if I inherited the Conqueror's. But'—he jumped up and raised his hand toward the sky—'I won't let it be lost, this realm of the Norman, as truly as his blood flows in my veins! This side of the sea and beyond the sea it shall hold together and rule the world!'

As he stood there before me, tall and brilliant, I could not turn my gaze from his splendid appearance. But he turned to me and spoke impatiently: 'Hans, when did it begin? And become worse and worse? In the hour, I tell you, when my father quarreled with wisdom—that is, with Sir Thomas. Don't contradict me!

'I am going overseas in disguise to the cloister where the primate is fasting and praying. He was fond of me and still loves me to this very hour unless every fiber of his being has become monkish. Don't interrupt me! I will go and embrace his knees. I will beg him, not as a king's son and not as to a human being. I will not rest until I have brought those two together and reconciled them. He must be my father's chancellor again, for only his great, unique intelligence is able to untangle this confusion.'

I knew how much Sir Richard enjoyed disguising himself and riding out for an adventure. But this time it was unfeigned, artless filial sorrow rather than high spirits that urged him.

I pointed out to the madcap how easily an unsuccessful attempt at reconciliation can turn into an aggravated enmity. But then I went without delay to get some rough clothes for him and myself. I was willing to accompany him, for his cheerful confidence had bedazzled even me, for all my experience.

There was no need for me to ask the king for a leave of absence. Since he knew I had been a witness of his humiliation, he would certainly be more than glad to do without the sight of me for a few days.

WE RODE across France dressed as impoverished German knights looking for service and pay in a war. Sir Richard's youth and aristocratic ways shone through the patched cloak so splendidly that to avert suspicion I discarded my good manners, cursing and swearing coarsely in my native Alemannic dialect in inns and along the highway. Besides, we rode at night and rested during the day.

On one occasion in an inn, while Sir Richard was sleeping in a remote room, I encountered a man who had received from the spirits below a power over human minds. Like a dark angel of discord he could sever the bonds of nature and murder peace wherever he was, with his sharp sword and his even sharper tongue. Lion-Heart, in time, was to come to know him; but on that day he was still shielded from him.

While I was waiting for my meal, sitting in the taproom, I heard the trampling of horses on the paved entrance and the noises of an arriving troop of riders. Five or six elegantly dressed knights, bearing weapons suitable for a tournament, entered and called for a good quick drink.

They were southern French, supple, with fiery glances and rapid speech. I soon learned that they were coming from a joust in the famous city of Paris; they had fled as a result of a violent quarrel that had suddenly flared up.

They had logs thrown on the fire and sat down around the fireplace, joking and exchanging witty remarks. The words leapt back and forth like swordplay in a duel. Some of the young fellows disparaged the women of Paris compared with the beauties of Arles and Tarascon. Others got angry all over again about the quarrel that had embittered and cut short the festival.

I could be in no doubt about who had started the trouble. He jumped up from his seat in their midst. With fiery eyes and tossing his hair he took command of the conversation.

'It is true! Wherever I go, flames shoot up out of the earth,' he shouted to them, 'high and honest flames, no smothered fire like yours. You hate them too, but in silence, you Provençals and Aquitanians, children of the sun. You hate them, those northerners with their limbs encased in armor and their stiff gestures, their domineering talk and their greedy eyes. You feel how they envy you your blessings, your hills flowing with oil and honey, the ancient liberty of your Roman cities, your favored ports where the goods and ideas of all the world are exchanged, your sea, your sky, your perfect women, your sweetest of all languages! You feel how they will force you out of the sunlight and trample you underfoot like vermin!

'For it will be so! The peoples of earth are exterminating each other, and hatred is the all-powerful king of the earth! But you don't want to be disturbed—so go ahead and build your nests, be at ease and have your fun in the realm of illusion, you sonneteers! Worship love, until you find the hate that is in love!

'But let me rise above the appearance into the essence of things. Long live Hate, the burning breath of the world! See this heart, the vessel of Hate's glorious flame! Whoever wants to learn to hate, let him make his pilgrimage to the blazing heart of Bertran de Born! Before this altar, hidden convictions become manifest, and hands move toward swords.'

And he pointed to the flaming heart in delicate embroidery of gold and crimson on the left side of his black tight-fitting doublet.

One youngster, who was ostentatiously wearing violet —no doubt his lady's color—spoke with mock timidity. 'I had a different interpretation for that little heart on your doublet, Sir Bertran. You have let your glances fall lovingly on ladies, even if only ladies of princely rank. Not long since you fared across the sea to your old flame, Queen Eleanor. Will you be kind enough to sing for us the battle song that you murmured in the twilight to King Henry's virtuous spouse?'

'That is not something to be sung or spoken,' the fierce poet sneered. 'I whispered to her *The seed is sown!* and to the young king *There will be harvests of blood!*

'By Lucifer's wings, I will entangle King Henry and his sons in the coils of a dragon, more venomous than the one which crushed the priest Laocoon and his children!'

I could not take my eyes off the man, who—to my horror—extended his arms in a greeting as he turned toward the direction in which we were to ride to the cloister.

Do not be surprised. I knew who it was that he saw there. 'There is one praying there who hates even better than I do!' he shouted. 'Greetings, comrade!' And he solemnly drained a full goblet to that distant one whom he saw in his mind's eye. 'You quiet, slowly digging man! You are suffering like your master, and like him you are letting yourself be killed. You think you are serving love, but hate is mightier; and your death, like that of your God, is the damnation of mankind!

'Bishop! Here is a wager: Which of us will plunge King Henry of England deeper into hell? I will find him there, and with my knee on his throat I will sing such a song of triumph that the circles of hell will expand, the damned souls will grow gigantically; and heaven and hell will vanish into nothingness.'

This hideous blasphemy, denying that the gentle pelican had plucked open her breast for the love and salvation of us all, made my hair stand on end. The Provençal noblemen, accustomed to such heretical jesting, did not take it seriously. Instead, they were making guesses about who Sir Bertran's comrade in hatred might be.

The conversation turned to a strange portent that had recently frightened the citizens of Arles. In the Roman marketplace the marble head of a girl had come to light. The eyes were closed; the mouth bore the expression of the bitterness of death. The braided locks, looked at more closely, were seen to be hissing vipers. It was thought that this mournful head betokened a coming plague in their sunny land.

All this talk of future distress and the present misery of my king so touched my heart that I could not help sighing dolefully. The gentlemen had paid no attention to me before, but now they looked around at me with some surprise. I left my goblet and went out past them with a heavy horseman's tread and a good honest Swabian greeting. They replied with pleasant nods, unhesitatingly and politely. But when I followed them with my eyes from the upper story where I went to waken Prince Richard, I saw them get into their saddles swiftly and leave as stormily as they had come; the headstrong leader was making some frivolous joke about my Swabian groan, and the noblemen rode off amid a shrill burst of sharp French laughter."

THE PROPER Sir Burkhard had repeatedly crossed himself at the stranger's blasphemies. Now he commented reflectively: "From the murky sulphurous stench of those words, Hans, it must have been easy for you to recognize who was sitting there with you in that French taproom. I am in no doubt who possessed and inspired that traveler. No other and no better than the fiend, who is a rebel and murderer from start to finish.

"That is how he knew in advance about the martyrdom of Sir Thomas. And I fear that his prediction may come to pass as far as the devastation of those southern lands is concerned, a devastation of which the terrifying excavated woman may possibly be an intimation.

"Those shores, I hear, are fairly crawling with heretics of every known kind, especially the stubborn Manichaeans. I am a lover of peace; I am well disposed toward mankind; I rejoice in forgiving venial sins. But in this case divine grace is being spurned, and truly I could not hold it against the spiritual and secular lords if they joined in removing these impenitents from Christendom, so that their abode would know them no longer.

"But it is better not to linger over these sad matters. Hans, tell me if Prince Richard's journey was blest. He is the only one of your Englishmen in whom I can take pleasure."

THE ARMORER was glad to continue. "I could scarcely keep my horse up with Lion-Heart's cream-colored steed. His yearning to see Sir Thomas grew from hour to hour. It was hardly to be kept in check as the towers of the monastery where the bishop had found shelter grew against the clear blue autumn sky and its walls gleamed like those of the heavenly city.

I knew my Lion-Heart and the strength of his feelings. I begged the prince to let me ride ahead and reconnoiter. He complained and objected, but reluctantly he agreed.

The brother at the gate heard my request without suspecting anything wrong. When I named Sir Thomas, he replied with respectful gestures and a devout countenance which made it clear that here the chancellor was held in the highest reverence and the odor of sanctity. He told me that the primate was in the church, and he would not dare to commit the sin of disturbing him in his worship.

Meanwhile the monk showed me the bare cell of the man who had been expelled from the episcopal palace in Canterbury. There were the rough field stones on which he rested his head while he slept. The hard cushion astonished me, because I knew the sensitive constitution and the delicacy of the chancellor's body. At last, when nothing happened and the holy man's worship did not end, the porter let me enter the church in return for my promise to be silent and withdrawn and do nothing to attract attention as long as the praying worshiper did not notice me. So I walked carefully between the pillars and immediately caught sight of Sir Thomas, who stood in a high-backed choir stall, pondering rather than praying. Since I had not seen that amazing man for some years, I was frightened by the unnatural thinness of his face and his deep, hurt eyes, which seemed to be looking inward more than toward the outer world.

I knelt in the shadow of the high altar on the steps and venerated the Host, without losing sight of Sir Thomas. I was uncertain whether he was aware of my presence, for he was entirely motionless.

When I slowly rose from my knees after a rather long time, the chancellor, without looking at me and with no change in his expression, asked: 'How is my lord and king?' It was in the same tone as when he used to ask me, as he met me on the threshold of the king's bedchamber in Windsor. Hot tears came into my eyes.

Quietly he moved down the steps and motioned with his hand for me to follow him. He moved—almost floated—into the cloister garden, a pleasant green quadrangle with blooming rose bushes within an artistic ambulatory in the newest architectural style. Although outside the leaves were falling, the natural fading and dying found no entry here in this sheltered green rectangle tended by painstaking monks.

The primate sank down on a stone bench amid the luxuriant shrubbery and repeated his question: 'How are things with my lord and king?'

'Sir Thomas,' I said, 'what he is undergoing is the common fate of human beings, but his is even more miserable than the usual fate. You would hardly recognize him. If you saw him, you would grieve over the sight, and your whole being would feel compassion for him!' I depicted movingly the deterioration and the confused condition of a majestic prince.

He let me keep on talking, at length. Sir, he listened to my words without malice, but also without visible sign of sympathy; and yet he did not seem uninvolved or indifferent. Rather, he seemed like one hearing that a disaster had occurred, a calamity which had long been foreseen and for which one is mentally prepared.

He said nothing, but I thought I could feel that his heart was softening. So I took my courage in my hands and implored him: 'Sir Thomas, you are a holy man and a Christian; you have mortified yourself in penance. If you could forgive the way Sir Henry sinned against you— things must yet come to a good end.'

But still he said nothing.

'Forgive the king,' I cried out again, 'for the loss of Grace!'

Sir Thomas's head sank and he answered enigmatically: 'Sad, if sweet Grace were lost—God forbid!'

AT THIS moment we heard the monks wailing and up-braiding a young horseman they were holding by the arms. He had taken the porter by surprise and invaded the cloister. It was Prince Richard. The long waiting and being incognito had probably vexed Lion-Heart unbear-ably.

Shaking off the monks, he fell at the feet of the primate and cried: 'Father! My father! They don't want to let me come to you.'

For a while Sir Thomas looked at him in silence. Then with a gentle hand he stroked the sweaty, disheveled blond hair from the prince's forehead and smoothed it like a mother.

When I saw this sign of tender affection I considered our mission a success; I discreetly withdrew under the vault-ing of the corridor, leaving the two men to their guardian angels and patron saints.

I sat down on a broad stone slab under the arch of a window opening which was bisected by a thin marble rod and kept watch, observing the two men from time to time. This ambulatory was full of statuary and, as I said, built in the latest style. Its pillars were crowned with rich moldings on which there rested, alternately, creatures from the upper and the lower regions—here a harp-playing angel, there a ridiculous or maliciously grinning gargoyle. I paid little attention to this ornamentation; my eyes were drawn again and again to that stone bench in the garden.

The prince embraced the knees of the chancellor, who seemed to resist only gently, until Sir Richard made his final entreaty, clasping the primate still more warmly; then Sir Thomas turned aside, sadly. But the prince gave him no rest until he had granted this, too. During this struggle for his father's soul the youth repeatedly spoke the word *baiser*. I guessed that what was involved was the kiss of peace; he wanted the primate to promise that he would bless the beginning of his next conference with the king with the kiss of peace.

Considerably later the two men walked past me through the ambulatory, hand in hand, the flourishing youth at the left of the emaciated bishop. I followed them. Sir Richard bowed over the pallid hand of the chancellor and wet it with tears of filial gratitude. In truth, my heart was jubilant too, hoping that the pitiable sufferings of my king were nearing their end. But alas, above the heads of the two, as they parted to go their separate ways, I caught sight of a little stone horror. It squatted on the band under the capital of a pillar, thrusting its little toad-legs toward them and sticking out its tongue. This distressed me, although it was a mere accident; I would rather have seen the two gentlemen part under the next pillar, where an angel was playing a harp and spreading its swan wings.

SIR RICHARD sent me at top speed to the king with a letter in which he begged him by God's wounds and for the sake of his own salvation to hasten a meeting with the primate which had been granted to his son's entreaties.

When King Henry learned from the letter that the bishop was promising him the sacred kiss of peace, he could not bear to delay in his castle. He hurried his knights and scolded his servants so that after a few hours we rode off posthaste—so intense was his thirst for the touch of the lips which would soothe the years-long sufferings and bring peace to his life, as he believed.

It was a gray day and on a gloomy heath that the two met. Sir Thomas appeared with a small retinue. He dismounted with some difficulty; he was of a slender build and had become unsteady, like a reed languishing from sun and wind. The king rushed up to hold the bridle for him, but the primate had already been received in the arms of his monks. He stood before my lord deferentially, a tired man; his eyes looked out from deep hollows and his voice trembled as he addressed the king: 'Sire, let the others step back so that our secret will not be overheard.' He motioned his monks away, and the king, obeying in haste, dismissed his knights, for he thirsted for the kiss of peace. I grasped the bridles of the two horses and stood at a short distance from the men while the others, monks and knights, withdrew about the length of a bowshot on either side.

King Henry could no longer restrain himself. With protruding lips he thrust his sagging bloated face toward the chancellor's ascetic holy countenance. It was ugly and repulsive, my king's face, but full of a touching yearning, as if he were seeking to partake of the Body of Christ.

What happened next, sir? What went on within the chancellor? Who can say?

It is my belief that this mixture of ugliness and inordinate longing reminded him of young Grace's death. He withdrew his lips from the king in disgust and shuddered when he looked at that approaching head, as if he saw the embodiment of tyranny and vileness.

But the king in his blind longing grasped the arms and sought the mouth of the chancellor, who repulsed him with a cry of horror.

When Sir Henry, with pain and anger, realized that the primate would not grant him peace despite the promises, his spirit suddenly hardened and he burst out in despair: 'Thomas, what have I to do with thee? Why persecutest thou me?'

The chancellor was now once more in control of his intentions and sure of his path. He replied with quiet grandeur: 'You know my nature, sir, and that I must walk in the footsteps of one greater than myself. I cannot be sure whether the Nazarene, to whom I belong and whom I must follow, could have brought himself to touch your horrible lips. He did kiss the traitor Judas, who sold him and delivered him to his death—him, who was innocence and love itself. But whether he could have kissed a mouth that poisoned the soul of his child and corrupted the body of innocence—that I must doubt. And since he is at the same time God, as the church teaches, he cannot forgive the murder of his lamb without a heavy full atonement, because he cannot destroy himself—that is, justice, which is his being. And I, a human being of heathen blood and not as calm as I seem—should I bring myself to do what my master would not have been able to do? And yet, let it come to pass! But for a ransom! Souls in return for a soul!

'Collect your thoughts, King, listen to me, and weigh what I say, for I have other children, your Saxons, whose souls you once entrusted to my care. How can the banished shepherd tend them in the pasture? And how can those souls thrive, when their bodies are the prey of your wolves, your insatiable barons? Since the time when your ancestor, the Conqueror, subjected many thousands of the vanquished Saxons to a handful of iron Normans, the victims no longer live on their own soil. On the basis of your barbaric hunting laws, you mutilate the men for killing some predatory animal, and you frighten young men and girls into the shadows of monasteries and nunneries away from the sun and the nourishing earth they inherit, which they should till and dwell in with security and peace.

'Do not stop me! Listen! I wish to create a people for you and the son who is left. I wish to prevail with the gentle staff of the bishop, not by conquest and violence, but through wisdom and justice. Since I am master of souls, I do not fear your Normans' swords. In these days of blind fury and clumsy trickery I am still the wisest of mortals.

'O my king, how foolishly you acted when you crowned your son Henry for the purpose of destroying my power! And how unjustly! For it was you who made me your primate, and I am your primate forever.

'Look at this'—he took a scroll from his bosom—'the anathema of the pope in Rome. He is hurling it against you because you have trespassed on the rights of my throne—an impure fire that I have not called down upon your head. Today the Holy Father is a hireling of your royal cousin of France, just as he was yours once, when I was serving you. You didn't understand the Latin mind and you were cautious about money at the wrong time.

'Put yourself back into my hands, and I will trample out this purchasable firebrand! I will also surrender the rights to my throne some day, after I have used them to get his due place and justice for everyone in your kingdom and create a people for you. For I am not a menial of the Latin, but a servant and brother of the Nazarene.'

At these astounding words the king's face was alternately inflamed and pale. At times he seemed convinced; then his royal pride rebelled against inclining toward the bishop or yielding to his wisdom. Hostility and dread regained the mastery, and his spirit remained confused.

'Behold, my foot is weary,' Sir Thomas continued with a weak voice. 'I am a flame that is going out; yet it seems to me to be a worthy goal of a life in this age of hatred and dissension to establish a nation where there is an end to beating and spitting in the face of God and man. Heir of the Conqueror, are you willing to be a just monarch? Do you want to die more peacefully than your ancestors? Over you'—and Thomas looked at the empty space above the king's head, where in imagination I could see a hand holding an unsheathed sword—'over you hovers a vengeance which is not mine. I offer you reconciliation. I am shielding you. I am now serving you better than your ambitious chancellor ever did. I am your friend! For see, your son Richard has prayed for you!'

Perhaps these beautiful pastoral words would have prevailed over my poor king if only the clever Sir Thomas had not brought up the name of Lion-Heart. For my king, although he loved his third son above all else, had come to suspect his own flesh and blood after young Henry's and Geoffrey's unfilial betrayal and revolt. At this hour it angered him that his son Richard had prayed for him, and a black distrust smoldered and seethed in his heart.

'Where are you pushing me, Thomas?' he began. 'Am I to infuriate my Normans? What are you thinking of? I should liberate my Saxons? Are your intentions honest? Are you trying to ruin me?'

He wrinkled his forehead like a man striving to think something through. Then suddenly a confusing rage came over him: 'I understand you!' he cried, 'you want to destroy me and my kingdom! Ever since the death of Grace—may God damn her!—you have been plotting my downfall day and night, you hypocrite, you vengeful heathen!'

Sir Thomas's eyes were radiant and his face shone like an angel's, as he said: 'I will forgive you for Grace's death and for your blasphemies if you release my brothers the

Saxons and from now on walk in godly and humane paths. Are you willing, King Henry?'

By now the group of Norman lords was becoming restless. It displeased them to see the king negotiating so long with the bishop, whose cunning they feared. Their reverence for their prince had already visibly sunk. They rattled their spears and shields, wheeled their horses, and shouted 'Finissez, Seigneur Roi, finissez!'

King Henry was alarmed, and ordered the primate to withdraw immediately. 'Back with you,' he screamed, 'back to your French monastery. And never again let your foot touch English soil, you seducer of my people! Neither here nor over there will I ever meet with you again or have any dealings with you, you sorcerer, you raven of ill omen!'

The last trace of life faded from the primate's face. He answered gently, 'I do not know if I can obey your command, for I have been wandering for a long time. Shepherd and flock yearn for each other. And I long for my resting place. So, O King, I do not promise to obey you. But you have nothing to fear from me. My footsteps are in quest of peace.'

'Beware of stepping on my English soil, on peril of your life,' the king yelled. He was out of control, and his gestures were so violent that Lion-Heart, who had been attentively watching the two while he waited near the Norman knights, came up in dismay at a full gallop.

But Thomas Becket turned from the king with a sad smile. 'I believe the hour of my release approaches,' he said. 'How else could a timid man like me have the courage to raise his head and anger my lord and king?'

THUS SIR Henry and Sir Thomas parted from one another without the peace they had both sincerely sought.

Chapter Twelve

"WE LEFT the gray heath, the scene of the refused kiss, meditating silently as we trotted toward Rouen, the fortified Norman city. After a prolonged warm autumn a raw winter wind drove the first snowflakes against us. Sadness weighed on me like a too tightly laced breastplate. For I had given up my king's cause for lost; I knew—as I did not conceal from Prince Richard—that the frozen heart which had begun to melt under the rays of a friendly sun had turned doubly hard when a new chill had come over it. I had seen with my own eyes how the primate, for Lion-Heart's sake, had tried to master his deepest feelings and touch the king's lips, and how he had not been able to.

With jackdaws and crows fluttering about him, King Henry galloped over the fallow fields, which were slowly becoming snow covered. Then, at a crossroad, Sir Richard gave spurs to his cream-colored horse, which he had been holding back in the rear ranks, contrary to his custom. He rode up to the king's Berber stallion and took leave of his father, with lowered head and, as it seemed to me, with a thoughtful and reserved expression which had never before appeared on his bold face. He pleaded some personal concerns and involvements in his county, Poitou. I understood that he would not raise his banner on the side of his brothers, but would stay out of the conflict.

KING HENRY stayed in Rouen until Christmas, which was not far off. He lived in self-discipline and Christian contrition; he attended mass diligently and subjected himself to suffering by fasting and every kind of abstinence, for he was determined to partake of the holy sacrament on the morning of the blessed festival.

He did so with reverence and joy. Then he sat down to a richly laden table with his noble retinue, to give pleasure to the stomach he had mortified in penance. The festive meal was half over when the Devil bestirred himself and sent a disturber of the peace.

Booted and spurred—for he had just rolled off his horse—the bishop of York panted his way through the hall. He presented himself, red as a turkey, with furious gestures, before the dining king. This squat, hotheaded Norman with his restlessness and vehement gesturings of his arms and legs could destroy the composure of a calm man in good health, let alone my king. At his side was one of his clerics, a reasonable man with a long face, who endeavored to quiet and moderate him with judicious remarks.

'Help me, O just King Henry!' screamed the short man in his high-pitched voice. 'As if the primate isn't enough to bear, the Holy Father in Rome has now aimed an interdict at my head. Thomas Becket—may God strike him with the plague—smuggled the edict on his own person into your English kingdom. At this very moment, during this holy joyous festival, it is being solemnly promulgated in all churches where Saxons are singing a mass, to my shame and that of my king. And in what manner did that son of evil come to Canterbury? As one celebrating a triumph, with horse and chariot and a long procession of Saxons!'

Here the sensible cleric demurred. It hadn't been quite that way, he had heard. For the primate had ridden on a gentle she-ass. It was true, however, that the populace had spread clothes before him and had strewn on his path whatever of greenery could be found in this winter season. The banished primate, he had heard, returned to Canterbury, weary, and had not left his episcopal house or even his room. The cleric admitted the truth of the report that the primate had brought to England two papal edicts concealed in his clothing. He threw one of them into the flames in his fireplace, but his belligerent clerics had snatched the other one from him against his resistance.

Sir Thomas was close to death, and soon nature would free King Henry from his adversary and tormenter. That was the simple truth, the cleric concluded. It had been told to him as the truth by a member of the primate's staff who was under obligations to him.

But the bishop violently smashed those sensible remarks to the ground. 'Thomas about to expire?' he screamed. 'By my bishop's cap, that tough man has triple life to harm Your Majesty. Thomas a bringer of peace? He brings war to England, war against you! Everywhere he goes the Saxons make disturbances and reach for their axes. I have it from eyewitnesses!'

That seemed to me to be impossible in the light of what I knew about the weakened Saxons. But I scarcely heard the bishop's ravings, for all my attention was fixed on the king, whose innermost self began to boil. In the confusion of his rage he paid no attention to the reports of the rational cleric. The blazing fire broke forth. King Henry, enraged equally by the insurrection and the humility of the primate, jumped from his chair in senseless fury and pushed his goblet aside so violently that it rolled clear across the table, pouring the wine over the linen in red streams, so that it looked like blood in snow.

'I have forbidden him to set foot on my soil,' the king shouted, his voice trembling. 'I know that he also carried in his garments a papal interdict against me, his king. He showed it to me himself, the evil man!' Then he crashed his fists together, despairingly, and lamented: 'I clothed him and adorned him like a mistress. He ate my bread, as a fawning little dog eats from a hand. And now this devil of ingratitude kicks me, tears down my house, destroys my kingdom.'

He looked confusedly at the party around the table and hurled at his knights the insulting words: 'I stuff food down the throats of menials! They gnaw at the marrow of my lands and stretch their legs under my laden table. But none of the gluttons and carousers is man enough to rid me of a traitor.'

The king strode back and forth, his eyes rolling, and no one dared speak to him. Most of the guests had risen and surrounded the bishop, besieging him with questions and reproaches.

Standing behind the king's chair I could see four men

sitting together at the lower end of the table, from which most of the diners had moved away. They were exchanging angry looks of understanding and were whispering excitedly as if they were conferring in secret. You know their names, sir, for the story has spread them throughout Christendom; they are the most wretched of all living human beings: every child in England makes the sign of the cross at the mention or even the thought of them.

They were, first, Sir William Tracy the scoffer, then Richard of Brittany, Reginald the handsome, a favorite of women, and last Sir Hugh the taciturn.

I was standing too far away to understand what they were saying, but their gestures spoke plainly enough. I can still see how Sir Hugh gnawed at his lip, how Sir Reginald wrapped his soft long hair around his fingers and tore at it, while anger climbed dark red up into Sir Richard's forehead, and Sir William Tracy, usually full of laughs, displayed a face distorted with the bitterest defiance. They seemed to have come to an agreement, and they disappeared together through a rear door.

I turned toward the window and saw the four wait impatiently for their horses and then swiftly mount.

ON THE EVENING of that evil Christmas day I appeared in my lord's room to receive his orders for the hunt on the following day. I found him silent and depressed, as usually happens with irascible people. So I dared to reveal my forebodings to him.

'This noon after your harsh, reproachful speech at the table,' I began, 'four of your guests'—and I named them—'rode off posthaste, I think toward the coast. If they read a wish or a command in your outraged words—O sir, what then? If they convert your speech into your deed, it would not be what you willed.'

He stared at me, collecting his thoughts with difficulty, and said nothing.

'By the blessed manger,' I implored and warned, 'this is no light matter! May all the saints and angels guard you against burdening your soul with a martyr!'

Now he suddenly understood me and seized my shoulder. 'When did they leave?' he asked, although I had just told him. 'Why didn't you warn me in time, you croaking raven?'

'It isn't too late yet,' I replied, unfrightened. 'Remember the snow clouds driven along by the north wind? It is certain that the sea is very rough and they will have a contrary wind.'

'Then saddle my Berber,' he commanded; 'he will beat the storm. Get the four and bring them back to me. You will overtake them. I wish it.'

'Sir,' I said, 'they won't listen to me, for you have stirred up their sense of honor to a fighting pitch. It is better if I take another route and reach the coast where the Channel is narrowest. I can requisition the fastest ship, no matter whose it is, and get to Canterbury before the four whom your anger has dispatched. Then I can see to Sir Thomas's safety in your name.'

'That is your concern!' he threatened. 'Know this one thing: I do not wish any harm to come to the primate. If one hair of that venerable head is harmed, you will atone for it: you will dangle on the nearest gallows!'

There was no need for this absurd threat. Never had a horse been saddled more quickly; no one ever rode more tirelessly. On the way I learned that the four were riding toward the nearest seaport, le Havre de Grace, as they call it, the Port of Grace. I hurried right across France to Calais. A fast sailing vessel took me to England in a few hours. Amid the plunging waves I prayed fervently to God's dear mother that I might arrive at least twenty Ave Marias before the four men of wrath. She heard, and granted my prayer.

On English soil I was frequently challenged by patrols of Normans in armor, for the country was in a state of alarm, and there was a widespread rumor that in Canterbury the primate was surrounding himself with Saxon weapons.

This spirit of uneasiness in the air made me ride on even more hastily. Bending over the flying mane of the Berber I drove the noble animal at a furious pace. Yet it seemed to me that the cathedral towers of Canterbury, which I was gazing at unwaveringly, were growing no larger above the houses of the town.

Bathed in sweat, I finally approached the walls of the city. I found the road in front of the gate strewn with pine branches and a few poor flowers, tokens of a peaceful entry.

I slid off the horse and led the panting animal through a back street to the brewery where I usually stopped off. I had often accompanied the king to Canterbury; its just-completed cathedral was considered a marvel of modern architecture. The master of the house, a Saxon, who was also the chief alderman of Canterbury, was just carefully locking the shutters of the windows facing the long main street. I asked him why he was shutting off the light during daytime. With his left hand he signaled to me to be silent, and with his right hand he pushed me to the wide crack of a window joist. I peered through and saw the four from the royal dining table riding up and down the street in full armor, pointing toward windows and housedoors with their swords.

'Everybody stay in his house! No one must set foot on the street!' Sir William Tracy commanded. He turned his black horse around in front of the alderman's house. The animal breathed out a cloud of steam into the cold winter air from its snorting nostrils.

After the nobleman turned his horse around, he repeated the order, not in the contemptuous way that Norman haughtiness usually addressed Saxons, but as a herald's solemn proclamation.

The frightened citizens obeyed. Here a booth was closed; there a wailing hucksterwoman carried off her baskets; farther down the street a frightened mother picked up her child who had been playing in the street and fled with it into the house.

The joking Sir William was unrecognizable. His eyes peered out under the black eyebrows, from a pale face, serious and unhappy. It became clear to me that the four had agreed on the way that they would purge themselves of the humiliating words of the king by a tribunal and death sentence, not through an act of murder carried out in anger.

I took counsel with the alderman. I convinced him of the validity of the king's real and final desire, and commanded him to encourage his citizens and arm them as soon as the four had left, and then wait for my signal.

Then I slipped through side alleys and reached the walls of the episcopal residence, where I was admitted as the king's servant and a person well known in England—indeed, gladly admitted as a helper in time of need.

I WAS LED into a splendid, pleasantly warm hall, where the primate was having dinner with many clerics and serving brothers. I hid behind them, reluctantly patient, waiting until the moment would permit me to approach Sir Thomas.

He himself touched none of the food. He leaned that ghostly head, eyes closed, back in the episcopal chair, listening to a poor devout man from Canterbury tell trembling of the entry of the four.

After convincing him that danger was near, the Saxon entreated the primate to save his life by flight. A frightened murmur ran around the table. But Sir Thomas did not stir. 'It is enough,' he said quietly; he blessed and dismissed the weeping man, and then spoke: 'Give me the chalice.' The young cleric to whom he spoke, a blond boy in a vestment that fell in soft folds, handed him a crystal goblet filled with water, which he sipped slowly.

Now I stepped forward and threw myself at the primate's feet. 'Revered father, I come from the king. He fears for you,' I cried. 'He has sent me by a speedy ship and on steaming horses to protect you with my body and extend the royal power above your head.' I turned to the clerics: 'Up, devout brethren, up! Help me! Lead your bishop to the innermost, safest room. And you others, help me bar the gates and barricade the doors! Once the first fiery onset of the four nobles has burned itself out and the attack has been repulsed, I will accompany the primate to the nearest royal fortress with the help of the people of Canterbury. Sir Thomas, in the name of the blessed Mother, do not refuse. Entrust yourself to the king's protection, and not a hair of your head shall be harmed!'

Motionless, the clerics all turned their eyes toward the primate. He totally rejected my plan with a few serene words: 'I know your master's will better than you do. I read his heart clearly. May God's eternal decree for me and the king's intentions be fulfilled.'

'By the five sacred wounds,' I shrieked, beside myself, 'the king has no wish that you should be slaughtered here! Will he bear the guilt if you defiantly carry out your plan to destroy your body and the king's soul knowingly and sinfully?'

Suddenly Sir Thomas turned on me and struck me with

biblical words: 'Get thee hence, villain and wicked servant, for thou art hateful to me.'

Terrified I jumped to my feet and retreated back among the clerics. I was saddened and even more angered that Sir Thomas, who until now had always dealt kindly and fairly with me, should in this moment when his inmost thoughts were bared call me such angry and dishonoring names, as though I had been the vilest of scoundrels all my life. Was that not unjust? I leave the decision to you, now that you know my life's story from my youthful days and I have concealed none of my failings.

Before I had recovered from the pain of that undeserved blow, the door opened and the four Norman knights entered the hall. They were without armor or weapons, in ordinary court costume. They greeted the primate with faultless courtesy but hostile expressions.

Upon their entry the bishop had straightened up in his chair; I was surprised at the noble dignity of his figure, from which every trace of weariness seemed to have vanished. He returned the greetings of his ominous guests with equal courtesy, and he invited them to the table with a slight movement of his hand. They sat down.

'How is it with my lord and king?' he asked, after a while, but received no answer.

'Is it peace?' he asked again.

The four kept looking at the bishop, some with lowered heads and threatening brows, others with nervous sidelong glances. Only an unintelligible murmur crossed their lips.

Then Sir Richard spoke. They called him Frappedur—that is, 'Strike-Hard' in our language—because of his invincible fist. 'We come in the name of the king.'

'I believe you,' the primate replied. 'You who are around him obey his signals and fulfill his desires.'

'Remove the interdict from the bishop of York or remove yourself from England,' Sir Frappedur continued, and the taciturn Hugh seconded him: 'Lift the bann or leave.'

'He has been placed under the interdict, not by me alone but also by another, the Holy Father in Rome. Let my brother of York apply to him; it is no longer a concern of mine. I seek only peace.'

Sir William Tracy continued the attack; he was the most skillful speaker among them: 'You cannot escape that way, you double-dealer with the forked tongue. Free the bishop from the excommunication that you have hurled at him. That burns him more painfully than the Roman one. Enough of hairsplitting and subtlety! Obey your king and liege lord in simple loyalty, as we all do. Aren't you merely a creature of his grace? Who raised you from nothingness and changed you from a Saxon into a real person? Whence comes to you the exalted authority of this throne? You malignant ingrate! Speak and confess: from whose hands have you received this authority?'

Sir Thomas shouted with a penetrating voice that vibrated throughout the hall: 'From the hands of my king, as a judgment upon him!'

This hard saying set the four into an uproar. Reginald the handsome wrung the fingers of his gloves that he had been toying with as he held them in his left hand. Sir Richard Frappedur shoved back his chair so that the oak wood cracked. The taciturn Hugh said: 'Finish it.'

But Sir Thomas spoke with holy majesty: 'I believe you are threatening me, valiant sirs? What does my king want from me? What is his, I am willing to give him. My body? Here it is; take it. My conscience, however, belongs neither to him—nor to me.'

Sir William said: 'Let us not forget the usages of chivalry. Gentlemen, leave the interrogating to me.'

He stood up, deathly pale, before the primate.

'Thomas Becket, do you rescind the interdict against the bishop of York? Speak!'

Sir Thomas was silent, and thereby sentenced himself to death.

'Thomas Becket, you returned to England against the will of your king and the decree of his parliament. Depart from England! Safe conduct is granted you to the coast. When are you leaving? Speak!'

But Sir Thomas was silent.

Sir William waited a while for an answer; then he concluded, somberly: 'That is treason. Your blood be on your own head.'

The four left the hall with measured tread. I knew they had gone to get their weapons.

THERE FOLLOWED such a silence that I could hear my heart beating against my ribs like a hammer. Then into that silence a vigorous voice broke out, a voice that I did not recognize at first. It was the voice of Sir Thomas, who was fervently addressing a crucifix hanging on the wall across from him: 'Prince of sufferings, come and dwell in this body!'

Again for a long time I heard nothing but my own heartbeats. Then Sir Thomas spoke a second time and stretched out his slender hands: 'Pierce them, and grant me thy passion!'

I trembled in awe and no longer trusted myself to look at Sir Thomas's face, because I feared the triune God had entered his body and was shining majestically from his eyes.

But I pulled myself together when I heard the noise of weapons out in the corridor. I rushed to the door and pushed shut all the bolts. As if released from a dreamlike spell by my activity, the whole group of clerics surrounded the primate. Some fell at his feet, others took hold of his arms to lead him away, still others grasped his hips to seize him and drag him away with loving force.

Meanwhile, ax blows were crashing against the door.

The primate refused to move from the seat where sentence had been passed upon him. But then a slender, intelligent-looking deacon stepped before him, placed his finger on his lips, and called attention to the faint ringing of a bell that could scarcely be heard above the tumult. 'It is ringing for vespers, father, and they expect you in the church,' he reminded the primate.

Thomas Becket rose, making no attempt to refuse. He followed after the cross that was carried before him down through the long corridor which led from the bishop's residence into the choir of the cathedral. I walked along too, taking my place among the psalm-singing priests."

Here the bowman stopped. He glanced at the hourglass, in which the last sands were tumbling from the upper to the lower glass. Hans reversed it and said: "Today is the anniversary, and it was at this hour of the afternoon that Sir Thomas began his last walk.

When he arrived at the choir of the cathedral he threw himself on his knees before the high altar. He was sur-

rounded by his clerics; more than one of them listened at
the vaulted door by the screen between the choir and the
nave and kept looking nervously through the length of the
nave toward the main portal, where any moment the four
Normans might force their way. The deacon had chosen
this refuge not for its security but because of the inviola-
ble holiness of the place.

I too watched that portal steadily, resolved that at the
last moment I would—not draw my sword against the
four noblemen, for that was prohibited for servants—but
shield Sir Thomas with my body, to try to avert from my
lord and king the guilt for the shedding of a martyr's
blood.

All things come to an end. There was a clattering and a
flashing at the portal. The four entered, armored from
head to toe, and stormed through the nave with bared
swords. Sir William Tracy shouted: 'Follow me, you who
are loyal to the king!'

Quickly I started to close the firm lattice iron gate
which separated the choir from the rest of the church. But
the primate forbade me with a gesture that brooked no
disobedience. He had risen and turned to face his murderers. His clerics pressed around him. The younger and
more courageous filled the steps. In front, on the lowest
step, Trustan Grimm stood firm, carrying the cross. The
others stood and knelt around the bishop, pressed together like a frightened and confused flock whose shepherd is being beaten.

'Where is the traitor?' Sir William Tracy called out. The
brave Trustan held up the cross against him, as a protection and a warning. A blow of a sword, a jet of blood, and
the severed arm sank to the floor with the cross. Then the
four attacked the frightened priests with the flat of the
sword and drove the scattering tonsured ones away in
terrified flight. I went to Sir Thomas, who was standing at
the high altar, opening out his arms like the crucified one
above him. It was like a double image.

'The king desires that you die!' spoke Tracy, and raised
his sword. 'Let it be done,' Sir Thomas answered. I clasped
him with these two arms, then I heard a shout: 'Away,
servant!' A blow like a thunderbolt by an iron mailed fist
that could only be that of the Frappedur hurled me away

and dashed my skull against a pillar. As I was losing consciousness I saw a sea of blood before my eyes and in it a dying smiling head.

I DON'T know how long I lay on the flagstone there. When my senses returned I was alone in the church. I tried to stand up. I didn't dare look at the body of the saint, which lay two steps away, in front of the altar. But I did see as I sank back again that my leather jerkin was wet with the blood of the murdered man.

Then shrill laments arose in the dark depths of the nave; the wailing grew and grew; the church filled with the poor Saxon folk, crying for their father and invoking Heaven's vengeance upon the killers. The figures rushed past me with uncanny haste and love to the holy corpse. They held his dead hands and feet and kissed the wounds, washing them with floods of tears. They dipped their ragged clothes greedily in the blood shed by the bishop.

I finally lifted myself to my knees, but my senses were still beclouded. I took a handkerchief and wiped from my vest the still spreading blood. Then grief overpowered me and I groaned: 'Mea culpa, mea maxima culpa.'"

HANS THE armorer sank from his footstool to his knees and groaned as he said this, as though the past had become present again. Sir Burkhard stretched out his old arms sympathetically and encouraged him with words of consolation.

Chapter Thirteen

By this time the scanty light of the midwinter day was coming to an end, and just then a dense dance of snowflakes was whirling outside the window. It quickly became so dark in the narrow room that the two old men could scarcely discern each other's features. A few little flames were flickering over the charcoal like will-o'-the-wisps, for both narrator and listener had forgotten to stir the fire. Now nothing was to be heard but the quiet snoring of Tapp, who was stretched out in front of the fireplace, and the nibbling of a little mouse that was busy near the breadbox. The canon's old servant came in with an armful of wood and fed the fire. An oil lamp with three spouts was hanging on a chain. It made a creaking sound as the servant lowered it. After a little while the lamp gently lighted the room with its steadily burning lights.

"I'm finished," the bowman sighed. "What more is there to say, now that you have seen that bleeding, battered head on the stone steps? What more would there be to say about the king and me, his unfortunate servant? Unless you want to hear how my lord went to pieces under the burden of that holy body which weighed more and more heavily on him—for even in glory Sir Thomas might have withheld forgiveness from him—and how that man, who could find no peace himself, drove away his servant as a hated accomplice. Even so, King Henry did scourge himself at the tomb of the man he killed, and worshipped him sincerely, as the chronicle reports."

"According to the credible testimony of my chronicle,"

the canon observed critically, "the king did indeed scourge himself at the grave of Saint Thomas in Canterbury, but not without shrewd worldly purposes; for he wanted support in his conflict with his sons and was trying to win back the hearts of his Saxons, who had deserted him. You yourself, Hans, have made very clear that your king was a great sinner."

"As a dissembler and a hypocrite, you think?" cried the bowman, shocked. Aroused to deal with this accusation, he continued: "By the thorn-crowned head of God, I tell you that no man has ever prayed more sincerely than King Henry, during that hour when he covered the feet of the saint with kisses and tears! A Saxon stonemason had portrayed him, lying on his tomb, his hands across his chest, smiling quietly. The man's art was small, but the statue was true to life, for he had imprinted in his memory the face of the primate in his lifetime.

I knelt behind my lord as he pondered and repented his sins; and when he bared the flesh of his back to the scourge, I felt the flesh of my own back creep. I too prayed ardently to the saint to follow God's footsteps and forgive those who killed him.

King Henry moaned: 'Only do not take from me the favorite, Lion-Heart, you mighty warrior of God! Oh, how little I knew you, you saintly man, near whom I, a vile creature, was granted the honor of living.'

A blast on a horn sounds. I recognize the signal—a horseman from the king's camp in France. Swiftly I throw a cloak over his wound-streaked shoulders, step to the portal, receive the message, and run back to the king with the letter.

I thought that Sir Thomas had heard him and at that very instant had granted him victory over his sons. He breaks the seal, trembling, but the letters swim before his eyes. 'Read,' he commands, angry at any least delay in satisfying his longing for victory and peace. But what I read was something very different:

'I Richard, count of Poitou, present a complaint not in my behalf but in that of my teacher and spiritual father in heaven, whose murderers still walk the earth hale and hearty, unpunished by any royal sentence or indictment. I denounce this negligence. So that there may be no doubt of it, I proclaim to kings and peoples that I renounce my natural father as he has renounced Christ and his witnesses.'

While I was reading this terrible document, hesitatingly, the king stepped up to me, his eyes staring and protruding. My voice failed me. He seized my throat with both hands. 'You lie, you scoundrel!' he screamed, and then collapsed.

But Sir Thomas, on his tomb, smiled."

"ENOUGH!" the canon called out, growing pale and extending his hands defensively against the bowman, as if to ward off further tragedies.

Sir Burkhard loved merry and cheerful things, as old people do when they have only a last remnant of life to enjoy. When he brought the bowman into his room, his concern had been to smile at some anecdotes about the human side of the saint and—in the interest of balance and moderation—to tarnish slightly the gold of the new halo. But Hans had shown him a tortured battle and two anguished human faces, and he was not able to cope with this sight. He tried to find a jest to blunt the impression. After a little while he commented: "It is a comfort to me that you are still sitting here in front of me with your religious faith and sense of honor intact. You are truly a flexible man if your king didn't grab you by the belt and drag you down with him."

The armorer had straightened up on his footstool, and his eyes were brighter. Telling the story had relieved him as a kind of confession and restored strength to all his sinews; for he was stalwart, despite his gray hairs, and he could endure the hard decrees of the justice that lies hidden within human events.

"I did not escape intact," he said, "but I withdrew in time, and I saw to it that I did not lack the help of many aids to salvation. I will tell you about that, and how I have become what I am, very briefly: the horses run faster when the stables are in sight.

As I RODE behind King Henry back to Windsor Castle after the scourging, it became clear to me that I would not be staying much longer in the royal service. Since the death of the primate the sight of me had become displeasing to the king, and he had reproached me with unreasonable words for my inability to rescue Sir Thomas from his murderers. When the king saw me, he looked away. A handsome page from an aristocratic Aquitanian family had supplanted me, the graybeard, as cupbearer. On the hunt, too, I seldom accompanied him. The only reason he had me ride to Canterbury with him was that he did not need to be ashamed in my presence.

In Windsor Castle Sir Rollo, the chief armorer, questioned me. The king's scourging had been noised abroad, and the report was making its way by word of mouth among the Saxons, spreading both edification and malicious satisfaction. When he learned the disgraceful truth the dark angry vein on his forehead swelled to the bursting point, and, in his fashion, he gave vent to his feelings with disrespectful words: 'He crawled up to the grave and prayed to the coward! How that bloodless scoundrel must have giggled in his cave! And stinging the king from underground, that is typical of the snake! A Norman king whipped! But it's nothing to be surprised about. Have you noticed, Hans, that for months King Henry has been wearing a priest's face on his shoulders?'

In this Sir Rollo was telling the truth. It was hard to recognize the king's face these days. It was disintegrating and sagging. In place of the merry radiance of old there was now only a dull glow like rotting wood at night.

'This English air is getting to be a stench for me,' said Sir Rollo angrily. 'I'm going to Sicily, the fire-spitting island, where a nephew of mine lives. Hans, take a piece of charcoal from the fireplace there'—we were standing in the armory—'and write a farewell on the wall there for me, and say that I won't serve any scourged king.' I knew that the noble gentleman could not write, so I did my best to put his thought into a Latin text that he approved. *Ego—Normannus Rollo—valedico—regi Henrico.*'

But before I put charcoal to wall, I remarked: 'I am making the same journey, sir.' 'What? You are leaving, Bowman? The king will miss you!' he remarked, and wrinkled his forehead. I pointed to the blue spots on my choked neck and said: 'For the third time I have brought King Henry disastrous news. Is it a wonder that he grows angry at the raven? My service brings him no pleasure any more. Why should I provoke his fury? I want to leave before in some evil hour he throws a spear at me like King

Saul. But your parting from him, since he esteems and values you as the oldest witness and embodiment of Norman glory, that will depress and frighten him as a bad omen.'

At that the chief armorer snatched the unused charcoal from my hand, threw it into the fireplace, and turned his back on me, grumbling gloomily.

On the same day I went to the king and asked him to release me. My heart was heavier than on that first day of my service when I showed him my improved crossbow. His look was not unfriendly, only sad, and as if I were a stranger. He released me. I did not become a rich man, but he had his treasurer see to it that I got my just dues.

WHEN I CLEARED out my room in Windsor I found the cloth with the blood of the martyr. I had put it out of sight at the bottom of a chest. What should I do with it? Probably it was more valuable than the entire payment that King Henry had allotted to me. At that time the slightest memento of Sir Thomas was worth a hundred, a thousand times its weight in gold. But it went against my memories and feelings to sell blood about which I was not without guilt. The other two alternatives, to keep the piece of bloody cloth or to destroy it, were equally questionable.

Before I left England I made a point of looking up my former master, the bowmaker in London. He had treated me kindly, and during the time I was serving the king I had kept my distance from him. He received me with many manifestations of respect, for he did not know that I had fallen from favor, and he laughed and cried like a child. Bitterness and affliction had weakened him in body and soul. I asked about Hilde. She was suffering from a wasting fever, he said, and he led me into her room.

When she recognized me, a light came into her sunken blue eyes. She thanked me for coming; she had longed to see me once again before she died. The old love rose strongly within me, along with sympathy, so that humbled as I was by the blows of fate, I suggested that I should take her home with me as my wedded wife if she could regain her health. She nodded, but doubtfully and sadly.

Then I thought of my precious blood-stained cloth. There was much talk and boasting throughout all of England telling of cures and miracles brought about by relics of the martyred bishop; even the dead had returned to life when touched with them, Saxon priests were declaring in their sermons. At top speed I rode to Windsor and back. I hurried upstairs to her room with my cloth. She was asleep, and I laid it quietly on her chest. Then she moved and gave me a friendly smile. Her eyes opened radiantly, and then she closed them with a gentle sigh. Sir, she was dead.

Fear and anger came over me that Sir Thomas, who could raise the dead, was relentlessly pursuing me and killing what was dear to me. I fled, and I suppose the bloody cloth was put into the coffin with her.

I HAD A stormy voyage, and twice the waves threw me back to the English coast. After I finally set foot on solid ground, I pressed onward toward Swabian country. The experiences of my life had completely driven out of me any desire to travel and any curiosity about the world. When I finally watered my horse in the Rhine, homesickness drew me irresistibly upstream to and through the gate of Schaffhausen.

There I found that nobody remembered the Jew Manasse. I was accepted with honors as a renowned man who knew his way around in the world. Before the glitter of my fame faded, I married a young widow, who in addition to two young sons from her first marriage brought me a tower in Schaffhausen and a sunny vineyard along the Rhine.

You will give me credit, sir, for not giving up my trade, although I was of noble birth and a former royal servant. On the contrary, I promptly opened a cheerful workshop which was soon supplying a wide circle of castles and cities with large and small shooting implements.

But about my king I heard nothing, beyond the fact that he could not be at peace with his sons or himself.

ONE DAY I went out to the Falls of the Rhine, taking along my wife's older boy. I wanted to shoot across the river with a new crossbow to test the extent to which the winds swirling above the currents would interfere with the flight of the missile.

Looking for a target point on the opposite bank I catch sight of a gray shape of a knight, sitting on a boulder, his

126

sword across his knees like your Charlemagne up there in his niche in the tower at the base of the Great Minster spire. My boy begins to be scared, and I rack my brains trying to imagine who could have put that natural-looking statue in this wilderness on the river bank, and done it overnight.

Then the knight slowly raises his mailed hand, and I see that he is beckoning to me. Now I recognize him, jump in the ferryman's boat, push my way across. And Sir Rollo shouts: 'Greetings, Swabian! I invite myself to an evening drink with you.'

Walking toward my home he told me that he was on his way to Palermo. He had arrived in this little city on the Rhine today and seen to shelter for his horse and his servants. Then, he said, attracted by a distant thundering, he had satisfied his curiosity by going downstream to this fine water display.

As we strode together through the streets of Schaffhausen and the people looked with astonishment at the powerful old gentleman, it seemed to me that in former days I had lived among an alien race of giants. Sir Rollo drank many a beaker of my wine and complimented me on it. Finally I risked a question about my lord and king. The chief armorer puffed out some air, and I understood that Sir Henry's soul had gone hence.

'And his dying?' I asked uneasily. 'How was it?'

'Without benefit of clergy!' was his answer. 'A blazing fatherly rage killed him like a bolt of lightning. Your idol, the youth Richard, had overcome him with the help of the Capetian. As a first condition of peace he had demanded a father's blessing, even though it would be an empty gesture.

'Then King Henry sat up in his sickbed, supported by my arms. Full of silent wrath he stretched out his right hand over his son, in a forced gesture. But the death spasm contracted the fingers in the midst of the false blessing, and they stiffened in the air.'

'Stop, Sir Rollo!' I shuddered. After a while I went on: 'With your permission I will accompany you a little way, to make a pilgrimage to the Black Madonna of Einsiedeln. I have to pray for my king's soul.'

On the second day we reached the barren plateau where Meinrad's cell is. Sir Rollo didn't stop here; he turned his horse onward, taking leave of me with a slight nod and spitting toward the towers of the monastery.

But I dismounted and walked to the shrine, barefoot and with bared head. After I had performed all the usual rites prescribed for purification, as a farewell I drank once more from each of the pipes from the spring which, as you know, issues from the blessed body of Saint Meinrad.

As I lifted my mouth, devoutly, from one of the pipes, I saw at the next one the head of a thirsting pilgrim whose right sleeve was hanging empty at his side. Then he lifted his head toward me, and we stared into each other's eyes. In an instant we had both jumped up and grabbed at each other's throat—Trustan Grimm and I. A powerful bass voice rang out beside us. 'Hands off!' and a florid young monk questioned us about our ancestry and homes.

When he learned that one of us had been Bishop Thomas's crucifer and the other King Henry's attendant, he found it excusable that we should try to choke each other. But he separated us with equal penance, assigning each his number of Our Fathers, and gave us an honest short sermon to the effect that little people had no business interfering in the affairs of the great, especially when those great ones had already found their proper places in one of the three regions on the other side: hell, purgatory, heaven.

So each of us went his way. I returned to my workshop on the Rhine; Trustan Grimm continued toward the Holy Sepulcher, muttering into his red beard something angry about the lukewarm Swabian priests.

AFTER TEN years the pope who is still reigning heeded the cry of England and Christendom, and exalted Sir Thomas to the radiant circle of saints of the church. Instead of the required three miracles more than a hundred had been reported and certified. Besides, the meritorious death on the steps of the altar weighed no less heavily in his favor.

When this was announced throughout the Christian world I entered Saint Thomas's name in my homemade church calendar under the first martyrs, the innocent babes of Bethlehem—with whom, to be sure, he had little in common except the violent death by the sword."

AT THIS moment Tapp jumped up and barked sharply. Soon he was answered from the street by the howls of hunting hounds and the trampling of horses. A harsh torchlight flooded the room. As the two of them stepped out on the wooden balcony, the armorer recognized who was riding down the steep street at the head of a hunting party. It was his patron and debtor, Sir Kuno, who now recognized him, too. While the young canon tightened the bridle with his left hand, he pulled out a full purse from his garments with his right hand and waved it toward the armorer as a sign of his generous mood.

Hans wanted to take his leave, but Sir Burkhard placed a shaky hand on his shoulder. "Friend," he said, "spend the night under the roof of Saints Felix and Regula! After all, the saint who is ruling here in Zürich today once called you a villain; and, unreconciled as he is, he might lay traps and ambushes for you on your dark walk back to the inn. Go now and settle your bill with Sir Kuno before the dice start rattling. Meanwhile a bed will be fixed up for you in my room. I do not sleep much, and tonight I would like to hear a living breath near me. For I am afraid that the bloody head of Sir Thomas might hover before me in the dark.

"Tomorrow, however, you can travel on your way confidently and unworried. Tomorrow is the feast day of the pious King David."